lonely plan

UPDATE
26

OIL
TANKER

Mobil

Update 26

Published by
  Lonely Planet Publications
  Head Office: PO Box 88, South Yarra, Victoria 3141, Australia
  Also: PO Box 2001A, Berkeley, California 94702, USA

Printed by
  The Book Printer, Australia

Photographs
  Richard Nebesky

Cartoons
  Tony Jenkins

Published
  May 1988

Editor	Sue Tan
Design	Graham Imeson
Cover design & paste-up	Todd Pierce
Proof-reading	Richard Nebesky

ISBN 0 86442 059 5
ISSN 1030 5459

© Lonely Planet Publications

CONTENTS

INTRODUCTION

The Lonely Planet Update is a concept that has grown from the Lonely Planet Newsletter, which in turn grew from the Lonely Planet travel guidebooks. If none of this makes sense, please read on!

Lonely Planet is an Australian publisher that began by publishing Across Asia on the Cheap in 1976. It has now expanded its booklist to cover virtually every accessible part of Asia as well as Australia, the Pacific, the Middle East and Africa, Central and South America, and parts of North America. See the back pages for a full list of titles.

Since the beginning, Lonely Planet has been supported by thousands of travellers who have written invaluable letters about their experiences. Prefacing every book is a request: 'Things change – prices go up, good places go bad, bad places go bankrupt – so if you find things better or worse, recently opened or long ago closed, please write and tell us. The best letters will receive a free copy of a Lonely Planet guidebook.' And the letters have poured in.

All the letters were (and still are) passed on to the relevant guidebook authors, but it seemed a shame that they didn't see the light of day until the next edition of the relevant book. So, in 1981, Lonely Planet began publishing a quarterly newsletter that incorporated letters from readers and information collected by other Lonely Planet travellers and writers. This newsletter was sold by subscription, around the world. The San Francisco Examiner reviewing the Newsletter said 'it is crammed with travel tips ... and it is captivating reading'.

The Newsletter was printed on flimsy paper (for airmail) and was, unfortunately, not suitable for shop sales, so once again the people at Lonely Planet felt the information was not getting the audience it deserved. The solution was to go to a paperback format that could be displayed on bookshop shelves.

Lonely Planet revises its guidebooks every two years, but during the life of a book, the Newsletter (now the Update) was the only place where new information could be published. This means that back issues up to two years old are in constant demand.

The Update will be published quarterly, and will be available from good travel book stores around the world, as well as by subscription (see the back page for an order form). It aims to help travellers who want to supplement the information in their Lonely Planet guidebooks, or want to stay in touch with developments, or simply want to reminisce.

Lastly, if you're a traveller, we want to hear from you! Tell us about your travels and let us know what you think of the Update. As usual, we're prepared to offer a bribe! The best letters will be published in the Update and rewarded with a Lonely Planet guidebook.

NORTH-EAST ASIA

CHINA

I got my visa in the Netherlands and it cost me a lot of money. If you're going to Hong Kong, it's better to apply for a visa there. Many travel agencies will get your visa for you in three days for HK$70.

If possible, go to the visa office in the China Resources Building on Hong Kong Island. It takes two days to obtain your visa from them and they charge HK$50. It's no problem at all to get a three-month visa and if you're going for a short while, they may give you your visa for free.

Tim Temmink – Netherlands

Having sailed to Japan and then spent five months there, I found the cheapest way to get to China was to take a ferry.

The ferry sails from Kobe or Osaka, on alternate weeks, and takes two days to reach Shanghai. It costs Y23,000 one way, Y43,000 return. It's a Chinese-run ferry, but it follows Japanese standards (so even the cheapest berth is clean and comfortable).

I got my Chinese visa in Tokyo. It took one week for the authorities to process and cost Y2000. I had to supply a return ticket and pay for at least one night's accommodation. After showing my return ticket, I cancelled the return sector. An obliging travel agent wrote out a false hotel confirmation slip, which otherwise would have cost me Y10,000!

M Spence – Australia

In theory, foreigners are only allowed to visit 250 open cities. The rest of China is closed. Cycling from city to city involves going through closed areas, but the authorities only seem to worry if you enter a sensitive military area. Unfortunately, they don't say which are military areas. The road from Beijing to Datong is closed for this reason.

It seems that prior to the riots, the authorities in Tibet were relatively easy-going in regards to where foreigners went. I have, however, heard about other foreigners being stopped after fairly short distances.

David Pindar – England

Canton

The *Bai Yun Hotel* has a disco on the 2nd floor. It starts at 9 pm each night and costs Y18 to get in. This price includes one drink.

The music is quite boring, but the DJ does have some Madonna tapes.

Gerard Yvanovich – Australia

Guangdong
Hainan Island

I went to Sanya via Guangzhou and Haikou. It's possible to go there from Hong Kong (two or three sailings a month), but there are also a few sailings a month from Guangzhou.

If you are in a hurry, you will probably have to take a bus to Haikou. There are two bus services: the ordinary bus costs about Y23 and the luxury bus costs about Y45.

The bus actually goes to Hai'an where you get a ferry (included in the ticket price) to Haikou. In Haikou, you can take the bus to Sanya. It's a good idea to buy your bus ticket from Haikou to Sanya in Hai'an. You'll probably have plenty of time in Hai'an to do this.

There are many hotels on the main street in Sanya and they all accept foreigners. Most travellers don't stay in Sanya itself, but head for Dadonghai Beach.

There are three guest houses at Dadonghai Beach. The large hotel has beds for Y10 FEC. Next door is the popular *Seaside Hotel* where dorm beds cost Y6 RMB.

It wouldn't surprise me if this hotel becomes more up-market in the near future. There are plans for hotels on Hainan to ask for FEC this year.

People go to Sanya for the beach which is very nice. There is a place called the *Sunset Restaurant* which served the best food I ate in China.

A plane ticket from Hainan Island to Guangzhou costs Y216 and boat tickets to Hong Kong and Guangzhou cost Y30 upwards. You must pay in FEC.

Tim Temmink – Netherlands

Shanghai

For a most unexpected night's entertainment, I suggest checking out the jazz evening at the Peace Hotel. I went along with a bunch of fellow travellers from the Pujiang Hotel. There was a small admission charge and, for a few hours, you are taken out of present day China and back to the 1920s and 1930s.

Wealthy business people abound, both westerners and locals decked out in finery I thought I would never see. Jeans, T-shirts, tatty skirts, thongs and runners were also permissible.

An all-male eight-piece Chinese jazz band pumped out the music as couples fox-trotted and waltzed around the highly-polished floor. Chandeliers dripping foreign glass dangled from the high ceilings. Drinks and sweets were a little on the expensive side, so if you plan to eat there I suggest you find yourself a wealthy business person to buy them for you.

Bernadette Heenan – Australia

The *Huai Hai Guest House*, in the old YWCA building between Xizang Rd and Zhejiang Rd, on Yan'an Rd, is cheaper than the hotel CITS will try to send you to. It costs Y96 for a room with its own bathroom.

Many foreigners working in Shanghai for any length of time stay at the Huai Hai. There is a reasonable restaurant there.

Miriam Lill – New Zealand

Jiangsu
Suzhou

I travelled from Suzhou to Hangzhou by overnight ferry along the Grand Canal. I didn't meet anyone else in China who achieved this feat.

I arrived in Suzhou from Shanghai at 6 am and went straight to the ferry office where I queued for two and a half hours, the only westerner in sight. If ever I worried about lack of attention in my life, this waiting game sure made up for it.

I was in front of the office window at 8.30 am and everyone around me seemed pretty excited at the thought of finding out where I wanted to go and if I would be able to go there. Some people tried to volunteer to act as go-betweens but, as no one could understand English, it was a bit pointless.

Eventually the window opened and business began. I announced the name of the town I wanted to go to and a volunteer on my side of the window repeated it to the ticket seller. I held up one finger and the volunteer interpreted for me. I said 'today,

tonight' in Chinese and it was repeated.

All the information was repeated about five times and finally a ticket was produced and local price was charged. I spent the day on an absolute high, thinking of what I had achieved.

I was the only westerner on one of six ferries tied together, chugging their way along the canal overnight. On my ferry, there happened to be a young Chinese man who had been learning English for eight years. He had never met a westerner in his life, though he had seen westerners in the street. Now he knows a bit about Australia and I know a little more about China.

Bernadette Heenan – Australia

Shaanxi
Hua Shan

This town is on the Beijing-Xian-Chengdu railway line. Not many trains stop at Hua Shan; most stop at Menguyan, and from there you can take a minibus to Hua Shan for Y3.

There are also buses to Hua Shan from the bus station in Xian. Apparently, foreigners are not encouraged to take these buses. Supposedly, they are for the Chinese only. We had no problem taking the bus from Hua Shan to Xian, and paid Y3.5 for the three and a half hour trip.

The minibus drove us directly to a hotel, which was near the starting point of the 'climb'. It was comfortable, but expensive at Y25 RMB for one person in a double room.

The *Jade Hotel*, even closer to the starting point of the climb, looks quite posh.

The town seems to consist of two main streets; one leading to the garden and base of the mountain, and the other going up to the station. The roads link up.

The main street is quite touristy and there are lots of foodstalls and souvenir stalls. There are few foreigners around and a lot of Chinese tourists.

You need light walking boots for the climb, a light raincoat, a sweater, flask, torch and sunscreen lotion. A sleeping bag is not really necessary, there are usually blankets and quilts on the beds. It's a good idea to bring a sheet along, in case you have to sleep somewhere that is dirty.

Food is available on the way up the mountain. Of course, it's cheaper if you buy it in town, but there's no need to stock up as there are lots of food stalls. The higher you climb, the more expensive the food. Take some biscuits along.

You can stay on the east peak in dormitory rooms for Y15. On the west peak, there is more expensive accommodation (Y21) in lodges. There is a wonderful panoramic view from here.

Technically, the climb is not at all difficult and mainly consists of steep steps. Before you actually start climbing, you cross a nice little garden (for which pay Y1). There is a small temple and another entrance where you pay Y4 (because you are foreign).

Ignore the sign which reads 'FEC for foreigners' and pay in RMB. No one will say anything.

We took three days to complete the climb. On the first day, we did the '18 bands' paved walk. You climb 500 metres gradually and then it's a series of steps to the top! Some of the steps are very steep – beware if you suffer from vertigo.

It takes five hours to reach the north peak and three hours to reach the west peak. You go through the Jingshang Pass.

On the second day, you'll reach the south peak, the highest peak divided in two. On the east peak, stop at the rock stairs and narrow passageway on the cliff. Thrilling! It's a pleasant walk under pine trees to the east peak from the south peak.

On the third day, visit the central peak on your way down. It takes at least four hours to descend.

Virginie Dameron – France

Xian

The *Xiao Zhai Fan Dian* has rooms for Y15. They won't offer rooms for any less. Across the street is a much smaller, cheaper hotel where you can get a bed for Y4 per night. Rumour has it that they even have showers but, as I was the only guest, I wasn't allowed to use them.

There are public baths down the street. In summer, when there are more tourists around, the hotel has a bath house for its guests.

Suzanne Thomas – USA

Of all the people I met travelling, no one actually liked this town. Apart from the terracotta warriors, there is nothing much to see. It's becoming notorious for its pickpockets and outright thefts. Be careful in the crowds at the terracotta warriors.

    Alex Matthaei – England

Beijing

Most people hire their bikes either opposite CITS (Y3 per day, Y100 deposit), or opposite the Friendship Store (Y3 per day, Y200 deposit).

    The best bikes are to be found near You'anmen bus station, a short walk west of Qiao Yuan Hotel. Look for the sign 'Here hiring new bicycles' about 50 metres from a bridge.

    Opposite the hire shop is a nice restaurant which has good, cheap food.

    Tim Temmink – Netherlands

Better deals on clothing can be found just up the road from the Friendship Store. Walk from the Friendship Store up Jianguomenwai Avenue, past the Austrian Embassy. About 400 metres up Kianguomenwai Avenue, there is a small lane on the left filled with small stalls selling silk garments, down jackets, sweaters, etc, at better prices than the Friendship Store. Bargaining is necessary.

    Gerard Yvanovich – Australia

The *Qiao Yuan Hotel* seems to end up with all budget travellers. The hotel serves a good and cheap western breakfast but service can be very slow. On the other hand, if you consider the way some people think they can behave towards the staff here, it is surprising they get served at all.

    Tim Temmink – Netherlands

To get back to the city centre from the Summer Palace, there's no need to take a succession of crowded buses. A minibus runs direct to Tiananmen Square and costs Y2.5 RMB – pick it up where all the minibuses congregate. Ask around and you'll end up on the right bus.

    Alex Matthaei – England

Guangxi
Yangshuo

The *Youth Hostel* is clean and charges Y4 for a dorm bed, Y5 for a bed in a triple room, and Y6 for a bed in a double room. Most of the cafes serve western breakfasts and coffee.

If you are missing your daily dose of western pop music and western faces, visit the *Hard Rock Cafe*. The place is run by two friendly young Chinese men who will happily serve fried bananas, apple pancakes, chips, coffee and alcohol, until late. The Hard Rock Cafe is between the long-distance bus station and the post office. At night, you'll hear it before you see it.

Gerard Yvanovich – Australia

Yunnan
Xishuangbanna

I stayed at the *Banna Guest House* in Jinghong which has dorm beds for Y6. The other guest houses are nicer but the Banna has hot showers.

There is not much to see in Jinghong itself. The staff at the CITS office are very friendly and helpful – two of them speak good English and one has a great sense of humour.

Tim Temmink – Netherlands

Xinjiang
Kashgar

The horror stories we heard about the bus ride made us glad we flew. It rained on the bus for two days, and the driver refused to let anyone get their stuff down from the top. Books were turned into a pulp.

We stayed at the *Seman Binguan* which everyone calls 'the 'old hotel'. It costs Y10 per person in basic rooms. Bikes can be rented just around the corner. CAAC is efficient, though they should be with only three flights per week to contend with.

There is now a map of Kashgar available, which you can refer to to make sure you're not being cheated by donkey cart drivers. On our way to the bazaar, our driver stopped three times and tried to get us to pay and leave. Carts are not allowed on the main streets, but they know ways around that.

The Sunday market is held across the river, between downtown and the Kashgar Binguan. The area around Id Kah is a daily market, no more busy on Sunday than any other day of the week.

The main Sunday market has a lot of sights that the other markets don't have. There are people selling wool, mounds of old shoes, chickens, etc. Vendors set up on raised earth platforms; there are lots of these and you can find vacant platforms to sit and watch from.

Id Kah mosque appears to be closed during the day, but there is a side entrance to the south, allowing you to see the place without disrupting the devout.

The people at CITS are friendly and anxious to practise English, but they can do nothing for the budget traveller except orient them.

We enquired about going to the Pamirs and were told it was a choice of taking the public bus (which takes a day and a half and doesn't have an official stop there, so you have to flag down a vehicle for a ride back), or chartering a jeep (which is very expensive). We stayed in town.

We found a small Chinese-New Uighur dictionary, with a green plastic cover, in a Hong Kong bookstore. New Uighur has a phonetic alphabet, based on Roman and Cyrillic, which was imposed during the Cultural Revolution. It is no longer taught in schools.

The dictionary enabled us to pronounce a few words, some of which follow in a bastardised transliteration: How are you? – *yakhshimuseez*; mosque – *masjid*; where? – *kheyerde*; guest house – *mimankhana*; good-bye – *khosh*; restaurant (and possibly hotel) – *ash-hana*.

Prabhakar Ragde – Canada

John King is currently working on a new book for Lonely Planet which will cover the Karakoram Highway. Here is the latest information on the bus trip over the Khunjerab Pass, between Kashgar and Sust.

The bus from Kashgar to Sust goes from Kashgar's long-distance bus station. A Chinese woman named Xia Liu works there as a liaison for foreigners. Find her first, to convert rumours into 'best-available information'.

The trip in this direction normally takes three days. From June to early October, a bus leaves every day; at the end of the season this is cut back to two buses per week, on Tuesdays and Fridays. The cost is Y77 FEC or Y100 RMB, and student discounts are available.

Bad weather, landslides, or too many empty seats may cause cancellations and multiple re-schedulings, usually without warning or logic. The best you can do is check frequently at the station, no matter what your ticket says.

The Pass is closed for winter by 30 November (31 October for tour groups), but it may close sooner on account of weather; and this is decided at the last possible moment. Only people like Xia Liu really know when it will close, and they will only know within a week of the closing date. In the two years the pass has been open to tourists, weather has closed it early both years, around the second week of November.

If the buses have just stopped for the season but you are desperate to cross, the Pakistani traders at the Chini Bagh Hotel may have space in a truck or may be chartering their own bus. Or you can hire a jeep from CITS. An overnight trip to Sust costs Y1162 FEC: with six *passengers, this is about two and a half times the bus price, and you may have more control over stops for food, photos and bodily functions.*

Going the other way, the trip is not just the reverse of this. Pakistani buses go from Sust to Pirali, the Chinese customs and immigration post. From Pirali, Chinese buses take you to Kashgar. The trip in this direction normally takes just two days because it's downhill. The cost is Rs 170 to Pirali and Y44 FEC on to Kashgar. Don't pay this fare in RMB. It is illegal to bring RMB into China and yours could be confiscated.

At Sust, the only people who can tell you for sure about the winter closure of the Pass are immigration officials and the bus manager.

In 1987, tour groups could only cross the Pass on the 1st, 2nd, 3rd, 15th, 16th and 17th of each month, because of road construction on the China side. The work is due to be completed by September 1988, but don't count on it. Independent travellers, however, were allowed to go on any day that a bus was running.

The trip is unforgettable, but easily ruined by things like uncertain schedules, broken-down buses, demented drivers, and the road itself – mud, dust, and a surface that, as someone said,'will leave your kidneys in your toes'. Keep a sense of humour!

John King – UK

Tibet & Qinghai
Lhasa

We have had very few letters from Tibet since the riots last year. This one, written after the riots, arrived too late for the February issue of Update, but will still be of interest to anyone planning a trip to Tibet in the next few months.

I was planning on heading south from Chengdu when someone told me it was possible to fly to Lhasa. To my amazement, it was extremely simple to walk into the CAAC office in Chengdu, give them Y547 FEC and fly to Lhasa the very next day.

Of course, the public security bureau in Chengdu denied that Tibet was open and CITS discouraged the journey. It appears that Tibetan authorities want Tibet officially closed and all foreigners out, but the Beijing authorities want it open for political reasons. This is how CAAC gets away with selling tickets to Lhasa.

I arrived to find 20 or so travellers in Lhasa, all of whom flew in from Chengdu in December. Since then, there have been a few travellers coming and going, but I couldn't say Lhasa was packed with tourists.

While you can only fly into Lhasa, it is no problem to get the weekly bus to the Nepali border (Saturdays) or the daily bus to Golmud.

Foreigners can use internal buses but will be charged double the local ticket price, so try to get a Tibetan to buy your ticket for you.

There is also a big FEC drive at the post office and other official places. Student cards don't seem to help at all.

All monasteries are open, except for Tashilhumpo in Shigatse, and the monks are very friendly.

Murray Spence – Australia

Xining

Most people rush through Xining. No matter where you are heading, you face a long train ride out of Xining and it's better to wait for an available sleeper, especially if you're going to Golmud. Unfortunately, I had to take this train twice.

I've had a few hard seat train rides in China and they weren't half as bad as I expected, but Xining to Golmud is a horrible train trip. People were very

rude (some tried for hours to set fire to a girl's hair), they all smoke and spit. A sleeper is the only possibility to keep some distance.

The *Binguan* costs Y7 FEC for a dorm bed and you can buy good bread and yoghurt at the market.

The spectacular Taer Monastery, about 50 minutes from Xining, is worth visiting. Buses depart hourly from Ximen bus station.

Tim Temmink – Netherlands

HONG KONG

China Merchants International Services Ltd, Sino Centre, 582- 592 Nathan Rd, Kowloon is a good place to get your Chinese visa from. The staff are helpful and will issue a three-month visa in two days, for HK$120.

Vacation Travel in Hankow Rd is 100% reliable and the staff are very friendly. I bought a ticket from Hong Kong to Los Angeles for US$320 on China Airlines.

Bjorn Thon – Norway

JAPAN

Since the yen has become so strong, it's getting harder to stop and look for a job in Tokyo. You have to spend a minimum of US$75 per day just to exist in Tokyo.

There is new company called Jobs and Working in Japan, and their address is Mogami So 2F, 15

Yaraicho, Shinjuku-ku, Tokyo 162.
They've set themselves up as brokers
for schools. When I wrote to them,
they answered very quickly and were
helpful.

Ed Henderson

Hiroshima

I work for NET IN (tel (082)
2221212), the Nippon English
Telephone Information Center. Our
information centre was established in
1986 for the purpose of giving
information to international visitors
and residents. We are a non-profitable
organisation and have been approved
by Hiroshima prefectural and
municipal offices as an
English-speaking information centre.

The services we provide include
information on transportation,
hospitals and volunteer guides.

Miyuki Moriyama – Japan

Hokkaido

Takashi Watanabe (tel (11) 6447381)
is interested in hearing from travellers
who would like to stay at his place.
You can use the kitchen and bathroom,
bedding is provided. A room costs
Y1700 per night in summer and Y2000
per night in winter. For longer stays, it
costs Y28,000 per month in summer
and Y32,000 per month in winter.

Takashi's place in two minutes
walk from Kotoni JR station and 10
minutes walk from Kotoni Subway.
The address is 3-11 Nishi 1-Chome,
Hackiken 1-Jo, Nishi-Ku, Sapporo,
Hokkaido, Japan.

Takayama

There's a very nice pension called
Pension View Lodge, five minutes
walk east of the youth hostel, on Rt
158. It's easy to find and is owned by
a very nice man, Jack, who speaks
English well. It costs Y3000 per
person to stay.

Mike Diederich – USA

TAIWAN

In regard to Taiwan's notorious
bureaucracy, two bad things have
happened. First of all, foreigners who
do not have a resident certificate can
no longer open NT$ bank accounts in
Taiwan. Foreigners can still open a
US$ bank account which pays no
interest.

This is a real hassle for all the
thousands of foreign students studying
Chinese in Taiwan. Fortunately, those
foreigners who already had a bank
account before this new rule went into
effect, will not be forced to close their
accounts, however, they cannot open
another one.

The second hassle is that Taiwan
will no longer recognise foreign
driver's licenses. Even worse, they
will not even recognise an
international driver's license, unless it
has been validated by Taiwan's
Department of Motor Vehicles.

I understand that they are really
enforcing this new rule, and that the
fine for getting caught without a valid
license is NT$5000, or US$175. The
car rental agencies are furious about

this but, so far, the government has shown no signs of backing down.

Now for some good news. You need a permit to visit some of the regions in the mountains, but recently many areas have been opened up.

In *Taiwan – a travel survival kit*, two types of mountain permits are mentioned: Class A and Class B permits. The government has now suspended all Class B permits. This means that all the places mentioned in the guide book as requiring a Class B permit no longer require any permit whatsoever.

Class A permits still exist and are still needed for doing Taiwan's most popular mountain climb, up Mt Yushan. Class A permits are still difficult to obtain.

Robert Storey, author of Taiwan – a travel survival kit, *writes about areas of Taiwan that few tourist get to see.*

Taiwan is 98% Chinese. It's also an industrialised, rapidly changing society. Yet there is another side to Taiwan that few tourists get to see.

We were heading for Chingkuan, an obscure aboriginal village high in the mountains. I was accompanied by Miss Wu, a Chinese student who had been to Chingkuan once before. She proved to be an excellent guide.

We boarded the bus in Puli, a large town in central Taiwan. The bus was loaded far beyond its capacity. All the seats were taken. I found a very comfortable spot sitting on top of what I thought was a sack of rice. It felt strangely cool. Only later would I discover that I had made a big mistake.

The bus climbed steeply. As we ascended, the temperature became noticeably cooler, a great relief. The banana trees and palms gave way to pines and cedar trees.

For the first hour, we travelled on a smooth sealed road. Then we took the turn-off to Chingkuan and conditions quickly deteriorated. The road was a dangerously narrow shelf carved out of sheer cliff. The unpaved surface resembled a washboard. The bus driver had to change gears frequently. The transmission protested, emitting ominous noises that sounded like marbles going through a meat grinder. To make it more exciting, Taiwan's notorious mountain fog rolled in, reducing visibility to about three metres.

We drove under these conditions for about four hours. I tried to be reassuring. 'Don't worry about the fog,' I told Miss Wu. 'I think it will clear up soon.' Then came the deluge.

Tropical rainstorms always amaze me. You wouldn't think the sky could hold so much water. Visibility was now about one metre. Still putting on a brave face, I told Miss Wu, 'It's nothing to worry about. A little rain never hurt anyone.'

The landslide completely covered the road with a mound of mud and rock about three metres high. In addition, the road, never wide to begin with, was reduced to about half its former width. The other half of it had slid away into oblivion. The road was too narrow for the bus to turn around. We couldn't go back and we couldn't go forward. It was about this time that I felt my pants were wet. I had not been sitting on a sack of rice. It was a sack of frozen pork and the thawing juices had seeped through and soaked my pants. It did not smell good.

I was beginning to get discouraged. Fortunately, the rain suddenly stopped. Since the inside of the bus smelled of raw pork and betel nut (third world chewing gum), I thought this was a good time to get some fresh air. Miss Wu and I stepped outside. The bus driver soon joined us.

As it turned out, our driver was a real character. He could sing and tell jokes. He had a great sense of humour, probably a prerequisite in this job. He entertained us for nearly an hour by the roadside. Then a large truck overloaded with fruit appeared on the other side of the landslide. Although the driver was just a farmer hauling his goods to market, he proved to be our saviour.

The farmer had tools in his truck. Picks, shovels and hoes were set to work. It took over an hour to make the road just barely passable.

We continued on. Darkness set in. The bus suddenly stopped again. Another landslide, but this time not very serious. Using nothing but hands, the passengers cleared away the mud and stones.

Chingkuan gets few visitors. Consequently, there are no hotels. When we arrived, Miss Wu and I were both cold, tired and splattered with mud. I smelled like rotten pork. We had originally planned to sleep in the church, but an aboriginal girl took pity on us and offered to let us stay in her family's house. Her name was Baguyi. She was young, dark-skinned and beautiful.

It wasn't the Hilton, but we were very grateful for the hospitality. Baguyi's home was made of bamboo, stone, and scrap metal. She showed me to the washroom. Over the wash basin was a picture of Jesus rising. I removed my clothes and scrubbed them thoroughly over the washboard to get rid of the pork odour. I hung up the clothes and then I scrubbed myself. The only other clothing I had to wear were shorts, a T-shirt, and a raincoat. Not exactly the best outfit for a chilly mountain night, but it would do.

Dinner was a barely edible rice porridge. But dessert was a real treat, excellent large pears. As we were to learn, these pears are the bread and butter of Chingkuan. Growing pears to sell in the markets of Taipei is the one and only industry in this village. Although the aborigines are poor by Taiwan's standards, the pear business does bring a surprising measure of prosperity, and many aborigines are able to afford such luxuries as refrigerators and colour TV's.

We were invited for a night out on the town. In Chingkuan, this means attending church. I knew that Taiwan's aborigines had embraced Christianity, but I was surprised to discover what an important role it now plays in their lives. Especially for young people, the church is the centre of activity.

Apparently, our visit had caused quite a stir. We were the best show in town. The churchgoers were especially curious about me, a foreigner dressed in shorts and a raincoat. It had been years since a foreigner had come to their village, and he was a missionary. They naturally assumed that Miss Wu and I were missionaries. They were surprised to learn that we weren't. They seemed very pleased by our visit, but they couldn't imagine why anybody would be interested in their tiny village.

The nightlife ended at 9:30 pm. We went back to Baguyi's house. Her older brother had just arrived home. He was very friendly and very drunk. This is one of the sad facts of life in the aboriginal villages. Alcoholism is rampant.

Farmers go to bed early and get up early. I woke up at 5 am to the sound of roosters. It was still dark and very cold. I went into the washroom and collected my clothes which were now dry. I brushed my teeth and shaved, and went outside to admire the magnificent sunrise.

The town looked totally different in the daylight. The houses were basically tin shacks. Sleeping in the street were some pathetic half-starved flea-bitten dogs. The surrounding mountains were breathtaking.

We had rice for breakfast. We hurriedly packed our bags because we had a long hike ahead of us. Rather than take the bus, our plan was to walk out by a different route. We said goodbye to Baguyi and her family. Although poor, they would not accept any money from us. Instead, we left them some chocolate that we had in our backpack. They insisted that we take some fruit with us.

Our hike took us down into a beautiful gorge, then up the steep side of a mountain. The forests were thick and green, the views stunning. We could clearly see Mount Chilai, Taiwan's most dangerous mountain and the scene of numerous fatal climbing accidents.

We had a full day of hiking. By 5:30 pm we finally reached the main highway. We were lucky to flag down the last bus back to Puli.

Exhausted but satisfied, I slept on the bus. I had dreams of mountains, friendly aborigines, smelly pork and landslides. It was a world apart from the hustle and bustle of urban Taiwan.

Robert Storey

. . . . .NOTES. . . . .

China

Canton The *Ocean Hotel*, 412 Huan Shi Rd, is recommended as having friendly staff, a restaurant, laundry service and TV's in the rooms.

Hong Kong

The *Sky Guest House* is great and costs HK$110 for an air-conditioned room.

SOUTH–EAST ASIA

BRUNEI

Bandar Seri Begawan

Yashin's is a brand new supermarket selling most goods you would want. This is one of the few places you can go to buy fresh milk, but always check the expiry date.

Around the corner from Yashin's is the best Chinese restaurant in town, *Lucky's*. Look the waitress in the eye and ask for strong tea, and indicate

your need for a beer. She'll come back with beer in a teapot. Perhaps other Chinese restaurants will do the same?

Alan Davis – Canada

Muara

Most of my time was spent in the Muara area, where my brother is stationed for two years.

In general, it seems that people are becoming more westernised and less willing to bargain for items.

Muara contains the largest concentration of expatriates and it is here that the best restaurants are. The *Anchorage*, formerly the World Wide Club, has an incredibly diverse menu and food is cheap. The bar stays open as long as you pay the waiter overtime (B$1 per hour) and drinks are inexpensive.

It is a club, but the people are friendly and someone will most likely sign you in.

Alan Davis – Canada

BURMA

Since Burma has 're-evalued' its currency, the following notes are no longer legal tender: K75, K35 and K25. I've heard reports that this move was designed either to hurt the Karin Independence Movement (who blew up the Rangoon-Mandalay express about one week after I took that train), or to strike out the black market.

It failed spectacularly to achieve the latter goal, and the Burmese people now so distrust the government, that black market rates have almost doubled overnight.

The going black market rate for dollars is now K35 to US$1, with K40 for US$1 being possible if you exchange really large notes.

On the subject of the currency forms, I eventually had to burn mine in a ceremony somewhere between Mandalay and Mamyo. I had absolutely nothing on it, and the discovery of a blank form would have done me more harm than good. I succeeded in not changing money at Tourist Burma by sharing a taxi out of Rangoon airport, and exchanging my duty free purchases in the taxi. I got K650 for the Johnny Walker and the 555's.

Life without a currency form is undeniably cheap and I lived like a prince, buying dozens of gifts with US$100 – but I can't recommend it. I spent the whole week bribing my way on to trains and boats, and into hotel rooms.

Life only became comfortable when I teamed up with another traveller who had travellers' cheques and a valid currency form. She had no cash, so all her purchases were at the official rate, . whereas I had black market money coming out of my ears, but no form.

We agreed that I would take care of everything that didn't need a form, and she would put hotels and both our travel tickets on her form. This worked well and I didn't have any hassles when leaving Rangoon. I merely said I had lost the form and was ushered on after a few minutes.

One word of advice: I met a guy who took in two cartons of 555's, selling one with his whiskey, and keeping the other to give as bribes.

A packet of cigarettes is worth well over a week's wages on the black market, and giving cigarettes as presents doesn't carry the same stigma as giving money as bribes.

The guy I met found that on presenting such a 'gift', reserved seats became available on fully-booked trains, and currency forms were overlooked.

Iain Halpin – Japan

Is Burma just old ruins and temples; touristy places where Tourist Burma wants you to go, or is it a place where you can study everyday life, travelling around by yourself and meeting the local people?

Travelling in this country is time-consuming and exhausting. You should think twice about spending two out of your seven nights in a train, trying to sleep on the floor, and ending up terribly tired the next morning.

During our stay, we did it all: Mandalay to Pagan, thank God we didn't go to Inle Lake. Nearly all other travellers were doing the same. It would be wiser to stay in Rangoon, walk, watch and talk to people. You can easily take a day trip to Pegu.

Pagan is full of old pagodas; interesting for archaeologists and, for ordinary travellers, impressive. Of course, Tourist Burma wants you to rush and you end up being absolutely exhausted.

We enjoyed Rangoon and spent two days there. The best cafe is *Nirwana* – it serves the best yoghurt with strawberries in all of Asia.

A monk took us to see Burmese dancing one day, and at night we were sitting on the balcony of the YWCA, listening to Burmese youths playing guitars and singing Neil Young songs.

L Howra & U Siikaluoma – Finland

INDONESIA

Merpati Airlines offers a 25% discount on all their flights for all people holding a valid international student card (the green one). At the same time you must be under 26, but I don't think they always check that.

I got two cheap flights on my card: Mataram to Denpasar, 14,800 rp and Jakarta to Medan, 104,000 rp.

Some good advice – when travelling on public buses and bemos, try to avoid sitting next to small children (no matter how cute they are!) as 90% of children will be sick during the trip and you and your pack will be a likely target!

Michael Sorensen – Denmark

Java

Mt Bromo

Having done the sunrise bit, a nice walk to get away from the crowds is to

THIS CHARMER SCRUTINIZED MY VISA EXTENSION FORM FOR TWO HOURS....

follow the rim clockwise, until a path branches off to the left along a ridge.

If you walk along the path for a km or so, you eventually climb a scrub-covered hillside to get a superb view of Mt Semen a few km away.

When I was there the volcano was puffing away every 30 minutes, leaving a smoke trail across the sky like a steam train. As most people return to their hotels straight after sunrise, you get this view all to yourself and can relax in the early morning sun.

Richard Tucker – England

Bali

We followed your suggested bicycle trip but, if we were to do one again, we would not go to Bedugul as there's not much to see. It's better to take the Ubud-Penelokan-Singaraja route up to Lovina and follow the east coast down.

A good way to bargain if you want the bikes for a long time is to show the money in advance. Our bicycle hire man refused to rent us the bikes for 1000 rp per day, but when he saw 90,000 rp for 45 days (two bikes), he couldn't resist.

Gunilla Swenson – Sweden

Candidasa

The east side of town is cheapest. The *Orchid Bungalows*, next to Puri Pudak Bungalows, are right by the sea and cost 5000 rp including a small breakfast.

Gunilla Swenson – Sweden

Kuta

Still the best place for buying cheap clothes and jewellery if you can stand the hassle.

The *Berlian Inn* is run by a lovely lady called Made. It's very clean and has a wonderful garden. Unfortunately, it's not very cheap at 10,000 rp for a double room with a big breakfast.

The *Treehouse* is near the Berlian Inn in Poppies Lane. It serves the best and cheapest food we found in Kuta.

Gunilla Swenson – Sweden

Lovina

The Susila Beach Inn has opened a new place, near the beach, called *Susila Beach Inn II*. They have small bungalows, each with own verandah, toilet and shower. A double room costs 5000 rp and a single room costs 2000 rp. Breakfast is included.

Next door, is *Tony's Grill*, a nice restaurant serving good food, and delicious sandwiches.

Cecilia Eklund – Sweden

Ubud

Two km south of Ubud is Peliatan. We stayed at the *Siti Homestay*, right next to the Sari Bungalows, for about 4500 rp a night for a double room.

The people are friendly; the husband being a school teacher and the wife a temple teacher. Their beautiful garden is next to a modest temple, and the priests come and eat breakfast at the homestay.

Peter Baak – Netherlands

The *Roof Garden Restaurant* serves great Indonesian dishes as well as pasta dishes. The place is very clean and beautifully designed with two stories of seating, a lovely view and reasonable prices.

The owners are friendly and courteous, and they have an excellent sound system.

Sandra Seidita – USA

Nusa Tenggara
Lombok

I climbed Mt Rinjani with a Dutch couple, taking six days to and from Ampenan, traversing the crater from Batu Koq to Sembulan. Without doubt it was the highlight of my trip.

We didn't have a tent. There are quite a few shelters along the way and, although it was very cold at night, there is a fair amount of wood around with which you can light a fire.

The first two days were pretty much as described in the Lonely Planet Indonesia guide. At the hot springs, I recommend going a little way downstream for privacy.

On the third day, we warmed up in the springs before having a three-hour climb to a shelter by the path just before the junction with the summit route. This shelter is just a hollow scooped out of the ground and lined with dry grass. A few old sheets of iron serve as a roof. It fits three people, or maybe an intimate four.

There is wood that can be used for a fire – useful, as the shelter must be at 3000 metres or more and as soon as the sun goes down it gets very cold.

The next morning we watched sunrise from the junction of the paths over Sumbawa, before starting the final ascent. The view from the rim is great, but it's nothing compared to the view from the very top! From the top, you look down into the crater which fills up with 'cotton wool' cloud streaming through the gap in the crater wall at the hot springs. In the distance, you look over Bali in one direction and Sumbawa in the other.

It's a difficult three-hour climb from the shelter; the air gets thinner and the terrain is horrible to walk on. It's powdery to start with, then you find loose stones on a steep slope (offering little support for your weight). It's a case of climbing one step up, then sliding two thirds of a step back down, and the peak always looks closer than it is! Climbing without strong-toed shoes or boots would be masochistic.

Richard Tucker – England

This is the procedure for sending parcels home from Lombok by sea. Keep parcels under 10 kg. Go to the post office and ask for the necessary forms: CP2 (expedition document) and C2/CP3 (customs declaration form – you need five of these).

You should go to the GPO in Mataram because the other post offices often don't have the right forms.

Take your parcel and the forms to the customs office in Ampenan and they will check your parcel to make sure there are no antiques in it. The customs people are very helpful.

They will keep a copy of form C2/CP3 and return the others to you, along with your parcel which you must pack and seal in front of them.

Return to the post office – local post offices take parcels weighing up to 3 kg and the GPO takes parcels weighing up to 10 kg. They'll keep all the forms and give you a receipt for form CP2.

Parcels sent by seamail take about three months to get to Europe.

M Denys – Belgium

MALAYSIA

Peninsular Malaysia
Kuantan

The *Tong Nam Ah* costs M$12 per night. It's noisy but they do provide a towel and soap. There is a laundry just around the corner in Jalan Mahkota.

Roy Vinnicombe – Australia

Melaka

Cowboy Lim's Travellers' House has moved to quieter, roomier accommodations at 168 Taman Melaka Raya. The rates start at M$5 in the dorm. It's M$7 for a single room and M$18 for a four-bed room. All rooms have fans.

There is a washing machine you can use for M$1.50 (soap is free).

If Lim isn't at the bus stop to meet you (he wears a cowboy hat), take bus No 17 or No 35 from town.

L & S Davidson – USA

The *Paradise Hotel*, 4 Jalan Tengkera, has dormitory beds for M$5, single rooms from M$8 and doubles from M$10. Tea and coffee is free. There is a games room, a library, a laundry, and you can use the kitchen.

Stuart & Louise – England

Joe Cummings is the author of Lonely Planet's guide, Thailand – a travel survival kit. He has also worked on updates of Southeast Asia on a shoestring, Burma – a travel survival kit, and Malaysia, Singapore & Brunei – a travel survival kit.

Malaysia's Pulau Langkawi, perched right on the Malaysian-Thai marine border, is an island worth exploring and can become a gateway to further adventures in Thailand.

A boat from Kuala Perlis in Kedah state on the Malay peninsula will take you to the Langkawi pier in about an hour for M$10. On Langkawi, there are several locals who do reasonably-priced boat trips to outer islands.

In the town of Kuah, where boats from the mainland dock, check with Mr Velu at the Hotel Malaysia. Mr Velu can arrange transport (taxi or rented motorcycles) around the island as well as boats to Pulau Bunbon and Pulau Dayang Bunting. Pulau Bunbon is a small uninhabited island with beach bungalows for rent for M$10 to M$15 per day. Dayang Bunting encircles a freshwater lake said by legend to be inhabited by a great white crocodile. As the legend goes, this crocodile grants fertility to any woman who comes and pays homage. You can also arrange boats from the bungalow operators on Pantai Chenang, which is the nicest beach on Langkawi. Sandy's Place rents bungalows for M$15.

A more exciting possibility is sailing a boat from Langkawi to the Tarutao group of islands in Thailand just north of here. From Pantai Chenang you can just make out the outline of Koh Adang in Thailand, one of the Tarutao islands. It's a bit like looking at Lanai from Maui, in Hawaii. There is no scheduled boat service to Tarutao, nor does anyone advertise a charter. But if you meet the right people, you can hitch rides with Malay fishermen going there. Good places to meet such fishermen are on Pantai Chenang at Sandy's Place and in the nearby village of Padang Masirwat.

A trip to Tarutao is, strictly speaking, illegal, as there is no Thai immigration office there. If you go to Koh Adang, no one will bother you. In fact, it's mostly populated by orang laut (coastal people) who have only a fleeting allegiance to either Malaysia or Thailand. Once or twice a week there are boats from Koh Adang via Koh Tarutao to Pak Bara on the Thai mainland for 50B.

A legal way to boat from Langkawi to Thailand is to take the daily launch from Kuah to the Thai town of Satun. The trip takes an hour and costs the same as boats between Langkawi and Kuala Perlis in Malaysia. The immigration office in Satun will stamp your passport, but you'll have to ask. The least interesting boat trip between Malaysia and Thailand is the direct service between Kuala Perlis and Satun for M$4 (40B in the reverse direction).

Joe Cummings

SINGAPORE

I stayed at Philip Coo's homestay in Bencoolen St. It costs S$7 in the dormitory and S$22 for a double room with private bathroom.

Philip's sister sells cheap airline tickets – a return to Jakarta is S$250 on KLM.

Scandinavians can go to the Norwegian Seaman's church to drink tea, swim and read newspapers.

Bjorn Thon – Norway

THAILAND

The Thai Vegetarian Subsistence
Movement, *Mangsawirat*, is quickly
gaining popularity in Thailand.
Sympathisers dress in blue farmer's
clothes made from handmade cotton,
and eat all meals before sunset.

There are restaurants which supply
high quality food at the cheapest
possible prices. Their aim is to
eventually convert all Thais to
vegetarianism. The vegetarian food
we ate here is the best we've ever
eaten, and the people serving it are
really friendly.

Mangsawirat also runs several
communes throughout Thailand, where
they grow their own food and have
their own schools. In any town, just
ask where the vegetarian restaurant is,
'*Rahn ahahn mangsawirat yoo tee ny
kap?*'.

Sixteen years ago, a monk named
Santi Asok established the movement
which is based on Bhuddist principles.
Thai monks now choose whether or
not they eat only vegetarian food.

There was not much response from
the general population until General
Chamlong Si-Mellang, from Bangkok,
embraced the movement in 1980. He
called upon everyone to become
vegetarians. Since then, the movement
has rapidly grown and there are now
more than 80 restaurants run by the
movement in Thailand.

The largest vegetarian community
is at Nakorn Pathom, 60 km from
Bangkok. It's called Moobahn Khlong
Gahn Prathom Asok and they welcome
visitors.

Oöol Fjölkunnigr – Canada

Bangkok

You should take the train from the
airport to Bangkok station. There is a
station, Don Muang station, opposite
the airport terminal. From Don Muang
to Bangkok, trains depart at 3.13, 3.50,
5.07, 5.48 and 6.55 am; 2.36, 4.44 and
5.33 pm. From Bangkok to Don
Muang, trains depart at 6.40, 7.05 and
8.30 am; 3.45, 6, 7.40, 8 and 10 pm.
The ride to the airport takes about 40
minutes and costs 5B.

Mike Russell – Taiwan

The *SV Guest House* (tel 2530606) at
19/35-36 Sukhumvit Rd, Soi 19, is a
small, quiet, family-run guest house
with a total of 22 rooms.

The rooms are very modern with
comfortable beds and ceiling fans or
air-conditioning. There are clean
bathrooms on every floor. Guests can
use the fridge and stove downstairs as
well as the TV and video player.

The family is friendly and helpful
and everyone speaks good English.

David Judah – England

I went to the Advance Booking Office
in Hualamphong train station and was
told I could only book one day in
advance. You can book train tickets at
the Viengtai Hotel.

Use 1B coins for local telephone
calls, made from any of the red and
white booths. Long-distance calls
(within Thailand or international) are

made from blue and white booths. The long-distance area codes are posted, in Thai, on the wall of the telephone booth. Dial 13 for operators who speak (or at least attempt to speak) English.

Bonnie Edney

Chiang Mai

We stayed at a place in the vicinity of Chiang Mai, called *Laen Tong Lodge*, 13 km west of Mae Chan. It's quite out of the way and requires a little effort to get there, but it's well worth it.

Nestled between a river, there are some beautiful hills and some terraced rice fields. Laen Tong Lodge is the most picturesque, clean and well-organised guest house we've been to.

It is run by a Thai woman and an Australian woman. The food is good and is served at round tables, which encourages conversation amongst the guests.

Numerous hill tribe villages are within easy walking distance. The women running the guest house can organise treks for you with local hill tribe guides, usually from the Lisu tribe.

The advantage of this is that you are off the main trekking routes from Chiang Mai, Chiang Rai and Mae Hong San. Also, the groups are small and the guides speak numerous tribal dialects.

It costs 30B to stay at the guest house in the dormitory and 80B to 100B for double rooms, with a short walk to the shower. To get there, take a bus from Chiang Mai to either Mae Sai or Chiang Saen and get off at Mae Chan. You then take a minibus from the main street to Laen Tong Lodge. The locals know where travellers are going and are helpful.

T & S Kelly – Australia

We went trekking for a week with *Singha Travel*, Tha Pae Ro 275, Chiang Mai. It was one of the more expensive treks at US$100 per person, but it was certainly worth the money.

Our guide took us to places seldom visited by tourists. We had to work hard (a great deal of walking in the mountains) but it was the experience of a lifetime.

The price includes all meals, an elephant ride, and transportation by pick-up and a long-tail boat.

The guide spoke English, Burmese and local tribal dialects.

N Stada & G Zwaan – Netherlands

We got ripped off by the tour company we chose, *Fantastic Tours*, on Tha Phae Rd (next to a hair salon, dental clinic and restaurant). We were charged an exorbitant price for a day trek and told it would include lunch. Lunch ended up being a cucumber the guide purchased from a woman on the street at 4 pm! And wouldn't you know, I ended up getting sick after eating it.

We were told we would be picked up at our guest house around 6 am. No one turned up. We went to our guide's office and finally left around 8.30 am.

He took us to the elephant training centre, then disappeared to get some breakfast. We thought we were stranded as he didn't return for ages.

Eventually, we visited a hill tribe. Our guide didn't seem to have any respect for these people. He took us into their homes as he pleased, and we were descended upon by women and children wanting to sell us their crafts.

You have to have a hard heart to say no to their expensive goods when you're sitting in a run-down shack. We didn't mind buying our token craft at the first house but, after the third or fourth house, it got a bit much.

Becky Smith – Japan

We stayed at the *Orchid Guest House* at 22 Moon Muang Rd, and went on a trek with eight other residents of the same guest house. The trek was arranged and run by the owners of the guest house. We left our valuables in a safety deposit box.

During the trek, the guide managed to run up large debts for several members of our party. Upon returning to the Orchid Hotel, it proved to be nearly impossible to get our money back and we ended up going to the police.

More importantly, some travellers' cheques were stolen from the safe while we were trekking. The people at the guest house were apologetic, but we had to threaten to go to the police before anything was done. They gave the travellers a total of US$250 in cash before the police were brought into it.

Fortunately, the theft worried us sufficiently to cancel our credit cards. It was through this that we realised what was really happening. Later we discovered that our cards had been copied while we were trekking. The duplicate card had been used repeatedly over the last two months despite the fact that the original cards had a stop on them. No wonder they were happy to pay the US$250 to avoid police involvement.

Stewart Browning – Australia

I went on a five-day trek with *Falkways* and it was quite disappointing. The entire trek was run in an unprofessional and inefficient manner. Because our guide stayed up late at night, smoking opium, we never started trekking until 10 or 11 am in the mornings and missed many places on our itinerary.

Despite the freezing weather, an insufficient number of blankets was provided – only one or two, rather than the three we had been promised.

I have since spoken with other travellers who have had similar experiences with this company.

Peter Heinecke – Hong Kong

The *Moonmuang House* at 46/3 Moonmuang Rd Soi 9, has double rooms with fan and private bathroom for about 80B. *Liberty House*, 22 Moonmuang Rd Soi 2, costs the same. The people here arrange treks.

Chris & Paula – England

Richard Nebesky travelled for five years throughout Asia, the Middle East, Europe and North America. He travelled in Thailand for two months and spent some time in a remote village.

Many people use Chiang Mai as the base for their treks to visit the hill tribe people. Few people get to experience village life. Thanks to my Thai friend, who lives in the small town of Fang, I was given a chance to stay in a Red Lahu village.

The village was a brisk and sweaty four-hour walk from the nearest dirt road serviced by Datsun pick-up trucks. It consisted of grass and bamboo huts in a small valley surrounded by jungle and guarded by dogs (not a very nice welcoming committee). The kids who followed me, however, were armed with curiosity.

It was getting dark so I went to wash in the local creek. There was a plastic pipe protruding from a tiny waterfall and all you had to do was stand under it and wash. I had a small audience observing my washing habits – would I keep my shorts on or take them off?

It was dark when I returned to the chief's hut. Communication was difficult as the chief was the only person who spoke (limited) English. Hand gestures and smiles were the norm when meeting the rest of the villagers. Inevitably, some minor misunderstandings occurred.

During the course of the evening, the children found my hairy arms and legs quite intriguing since the locals are not blessed with this phenomenon.

Dinner arrived; rice, heart of banana tree, green vegetables, and a little pork with chilli. The only other time I had meat (considered a rarity) was when the chief shot a skinny wild chicken. The weirdest dish served was scrambled eggs with fried bees. The bees had been smoked in a forest fire and made a bland meal.

In each house, the cooking was done on an open fire in the centre of the kitchen. The fireplace was built over a dirt base. As there was no chimney, all the smoke escaped from the half-metre gap between the walls and the ceiling.

The huts were simple bamboo constructions with thatched roofs and bamboo floors which had two-centimetre gaps between each plank. Garbage was dropped through these gaps to the pigs below the hut. There was no TV and no electricity, only small oil lamps. The toilets were truly outside. You just went in the bushes and the pigs took care of the rest.

The working day started before sunrise, with men and women working in the fields, or hunting, and the elders doing chores in the village, like cleaning up, thrashing rice or collecting wood. The children stayed with the elders. The villagers were fully self-sufficient and the *money they bought luxuries with came from the sales of opium and handicrafts.*

The law of nature applied in this village: animals were mistreated; the stronger kids dominated the weaker. When outside the village, all the men carried rifles, most of which were home-made and used for hunting.

The chief let me use his home-made rifle loaded with buckshot, and it was like firing an antique weapon. There was nothing to hunt but birds as everything else had been exterminated long ago. One day, while walking through the jungle, we found some rare deer tracks in the mud. The next day a hunting party was organised and the deer was dead by nightfall.

The villagers were fascinated by iodine, thinking it was some miracle cure. They came to me for treatment of deep cuts and, more commonly, leech wounds which they had scratched into big bleeding wounds.

During my last day, the chief dressed his four children in traditional tribal clothes so I could photograph them (they wanted copies of course). Their clothes were made from heavily-embroidered black cloth, decorated with Indian coins dating from the early 1900s.

On the morning of my departure, we got up when it was still dark outside. I left the village with the chief just before sunrise so we did not have to walk in the midday sun. It was a magical morning with fog still covering the peaks of the surrounding hills, birds singing and insects buzzing. It was a pity I had to leave this quaint paradise.

Richard Nebesky

Kalasin

The bus from Sakhon Nakon costs 26B. You pass through the Pau Pan mountains and you can get off at Phu Pan National Park.

At the park, you can camp or stay in expensive government bungalows. About one hour later, you pass a large lake at Ban Kumperm. Here you can stay at the local *wat*, but you should leave a donation.

Kalasin is a pleasant town and has a college of dramatic arts, where people study Issan music, dance and drama.

There is an interesting irrigation project which has created a gigantic shallow lake. There is a small river winding through this side of town, and many scenic wooden bridges.

The cheapest place to stay is at the *Kalasin Hotel*, an old wooden Chinese hotel. A single room costs 50B without a fan and 60B with a fan. It's a bit dark and dingy.

The *Saengtawng Hotel* costs 70B for a single room with fan and shower. It's very comfortable and fairly quiet.

Oöol Fjölkunnigr – Canada

Kanchanaburi

There is a chap called Pirom who organises small trips to outlying tribal villages which are very interesting. You can try betel nut, and get an idea of life in the villages.

Pirom is a social worker, so he knows the people and their customs, and he is very knowledgeable about their traditions, etc.

You can contact Pirom through the guest houses in town.

Iain Halpin – Japan

River Kwai Noi

The valley of the River Kwai Noi, upstream from Kanchanaburi is an exciting place to visit. Most travellers don't consider a trip to the Burmese border, and most maps don't show any roads going up to the Three Pagodas Pass.

The road was completed a few years ago and is cemented to Sankhlaburi, then a good dirt road continues to the border village of Phra Chedi Sam Ong, which means the Three Pagodas Pass. There are frequent buses leaving Kanchanaburi for a village called Thong Pha Pum (150 km away) and continuing to Sankhlaburi (223 km from Kanchanaburi). The road passes through beautiful scenery.

It is worth doing the trip by bicycle, as there is little traffic on the road and you can stop whenever you feel like it.

After Kanchanaburi, take the fork on the left and follow the signs to Nam Tok Sai Yok.

A few km after crossing the river, take the turning on the left and continue until you reach the temple (about one km). A long flight of stairs will take you to Phu Phra Cave. If you want the light to be on, you must pay 30B. If the door is closed, there is an opening on the right, behind a rock.

Don't miss the Prasat Muang Sing temple. Restored ruins of the westernmost outpost of the Khmer empire.

At km 60, on road 323, you will reach the Sai Yok Noi waterfall, on the right side of the road. Many Thai people go there on the weekends.

Forty-four km further away, is the Sai Yok Yai National Park, where the bus stops. The view from the little bridge over the river is nice – you can rent one of the many floating bungalows. Unfortunately, prices are exorbitant at 300B per bungalow!

A few hundred metres after km 107, you'll come to the Hin Dat Hot Springs. A dirt road will take you to the pool. This place is visited by Thais, so remember to respect the traditional modesty of the locals. Western swimming gear is not appropriate. Men should wear shorts and women should wear a sarong. The water is quite warm and relaxing.

Less than 20 km away, is A Thong Pha Phum where there are several places to stay. The *Somchaineuk Bungalows*, the *Rung Fah Bungalows* and the *Sri Thong Pha Phum Bungalows* cost around 70B per night. The best place seems to be the *Bunyong Bungalows*, near the gas station, where a double room costs 80B.

There is only one hotel in Sankhlaburi, the *Srideng Hotel*, in the first street to the left when you reach the town. A double room costs 90B.

Near the lake, there are a few simple bungalows for 60B. The nearby *wats* are worth visiting.

If you cannot find a pick-up truck going to the Three Pagodas Pass, just go to the intersection and you shouldn't have to wait long before a truck passes you.

When you reach the Three Pagodas Pass, there is a new resort with some nice bungalows where wealthy travellers can stay for 300B. There are only a few houses on the Thai side, and down the street are the very ordinary three pagodas.

A visit to Mon village, controlled by the Mon Liberation Army of Burma, is very interesting. The village is quite large, with many shops, and there is more food available than there is on the Thai side of the river. The Mon people are friendly and it should be easy to find a place to stay in a villager's house.

Philippe Longfils

If you're going to the Three Pagodas Pass, ask for Daisy. Daisy will put you up in a small house which was built especially for *farangs* (foreigners). Daisy speaks English well and can help you to get a permit to go further than the Three Pagodas Pass.

There is a village with a waterfall. The road up to the village is very bad. It costs about 30B one way.

Peter Bärtschi – Switzerland

Kho Phangan

This island is a half-hour boat trip from Kho Samui. Boats are quite regular and the island has its own pier.

The *Sub Bungalows* are recommended. I have been here for one month and know all the beaches and bungalows on the island. The 14 bungalows have been built on a beautiful beach in a wild area. It costs 40B for a bungalow without its own bathroom and 80B for one with its own bathroom.

Marc Statheld

Mae Salong

There has been trouble in this area recently. Most of the locals seem to carry guns. They speak a Chinese dialect similar to Mandarin, so I was able to speak freely with them. I celebrated Chinese New Year in Mae Salong and it was a very depressing event. Most locals feared trouble and stayed in their homes with locked doors, and pistols beneath their pillows.

Michael Fredholm – Sweden

Soppong

When leaving Tham Lot cave, there is a small plate guiding you back to the Cave Lodge. If you miss the plate, you can get lost on the trail.

This is what happened to one girl recently. After two days of extensive searching, she was found dead (strangled) and had been raped.

Do inform other travellers if you are going to the cave. Apparently, there are two yet unsolved cases of missing travellers in the area.

Barak Ron – Israel

Sop Ruak

Eleven km west of Chiang Saen, at Sop Ruak, there is an 'exhibition of opium' put on by the Thai government to educate the public and to warn people of the dangers of drug abuse.

At the entrance to Sop Ruak, we stopped at *Mama's Hut* which hangs (literally) above the Mekong River. 'Mama' speaks no English, but she served us cold drinks and was very hospitable. There's a wonderful view of the river, looking over to the jungles of Laos and Burma.

Janina Bara – Israel

Sukhothai

Finding accommodation is hard during the Log Krathong festivities. Travellers should book in advance. My friend and I were in Sukhothai the day before Log Krathong and we tried to get a room in several hotels, but none had vacancies. We finally had to settle for a room in the expensive *Rajthanee Hotel* for 450B. Later we met travellers who had been unable to get any accommodation at all. They had to leave town and miss the festivities.

John Barrett – England

. . . . NOTES . . . .

Thailand

Departure tax is 150B for international flights.

Bangkok Poste Restante charges 1B for every letter collected.

Chiang Mai The *Je t'aime Guest House* is a great place to stay and costs 60B for a double room with private bathroom.

'The grip'

"Gasing" — GASING IS MALAYSIAN FOR TOP SPINNING. A SPORT POPULAR THROUGHOUT THE COUNTRY, PARTICULARLY ON THE EAST COAST WHERE MAN-SIZED TOPS HAVE SPUN IN COMPETITION FOR OVER ONE AND A HALF HOURS ———

WEST ASIA

BANGLADESH

Islamic society causes problems for some Bangladeshi men who do not get to socialise with women. As a result of this, I was bothered by men.

Most men ask if you are worried about this and, to avoid problems, it's best to say that you are. Bangladeshi men treat women badly and think nothing of you having a pretend wife somewhere else.

There is another problem with young, educated Bangladeshi men. They seem to be too friendly. All you have to do is speak with one for five minutes and they think they're your pal for life. This becomes extremely tiresome as not many of them speak English well.

There are also Bangladeshi people wanting help getting to Australia, or wherever you may come from. They may be educated but there is no future for them in Bangladesh. At least, no career to match their intelligence.

Tom Kidman

BHUTAN

Independent travel has become more difficult in Bhutan with the 1st January restrictions on visits to sacred sites and monasteries.

The national museum, at Tadzong, Paro is still open but the treasury house of Rinchen Pung Dzong is now closed to casual visitors. The problem seems to be that tourists on group tours have been swapping digital watches and cheap electronics for local artefacts.

It used to be possible to negotiate a visa with the Royal Bhutan Embassy in Chanakyapuri (India), to obtain an Indian travel permit from the secretariat, and then to take a bus to Phuntsholing (Bhutan) and travel without the high daily (US$) charges.

This is now a hassle and it's better if you have a Bhutanese sponsor – difficult for first time roadrunners.

P Stevens – Canada

INDIA

As good old German health food consumers, we were amazed to discover *müsli* in India, and also amazed with what the Indians made out of it: museli, muesly, musel, musele, musile, musley, meusly ... and best of all 'spi museli choney pennuts' (special muesli with honey and peanuts).

Nevertheless, the muesli was very good and a real change from having 'bread better jam' or 'toaist burter jam' for breakfast. We really like the 'purridge' too. And one morning we enjoyed 'scrabblled eggs' and a 'tomotto omlet'.

Later on, we had 'sand witches' so dry that we needed 'leamon tea' and 'hot choklet' to wash them down with.

For dinner, in the more upmarket places, you are 'wel-comed' to start with 'horsd oeuvers'. Try the 'spring rools' or the 'frunch ounioun soup'. On the international menu there was 'Italian spagatty' and 'Chinees fried chiken'.

We went for the vegetarian meals and there were all kinds of delicious 'vegtabewe', 'vegtabiles' or 'veg-atables' along with 'noodils' and 'chees sause'. (We never did find out what to place on a 'veggi-table'). For dessert, we had some delicious 'pin apples'.

Bernd Herrmann – West Germany

I wanted to book a 1st-class sleeper from Udaipur to Jaipur for the next evening. I was told there were no berths available for three days. That's a long time. Has anyone else got a berth – the stationmaster perhaps?

The ticket clerk looked over the reservations book and counted the names very, very slowly. He must have found fewer names on the list than there are places on the train, because he turned to his superior, spoke the one magic word 'quota', received a one-word reply and I got my ticket. I did have to show my passport, presumably to prove I'm not Indian.

Louise Hope – USA

When I left England my travel plans were flexible. I didn't think it would be difficult obtaining visas en route and, with one exception, it wasn't.

In India, I decided I wanted to visit Australia and went along to the Australian embassy in New Delhi to apply for a working-holiday visa. I submitted a written application which determined whether or not I would be granted an interview for a visa. I was asked to return a week later. I did, and found that my application for an interview had been rejected.

Sleeping man – Manmad Junction 1st Class Waiting Room. 1am.

BUY YOUR TOILET COUPONS HERE

GENERAL .... 10 Ps.
WESTERN STYLE W.C. ---- 30 Ps.
(FOR GENTS)

'Ticket window' - Jehangir Art Gallery, Bombay
(CAN SEATS BE RESERVED I WONDER?)

I was stunned. Where was the justice in someone I hadn't even met, totally disrupting my travel plans and possibly denying me the only chance I would ever have of visiting Australia? After all, I was halfway there and this was my big trip around the world.

I asked to speak to someone in higher authority but couldn't. Eventually, I procured the telephone number of the man who rejected my application. Apparently he was too busy to speak to me in person (too busy wrecking other traveller's plans?). I phoned him and he told me the reasons for his decision.

I was penalised for having applied for the visa itself in that I had applied at the Australian embassy in Delhi and not in London. He said the embassy in India was only for Indians.

On my form, I had asked for a six-month visa within which I would possibly work at least three months. 'At least' three months, he said, was too long. Apparently, I couldn't change my mind now and should have given more thought to the words I used on the form. (Blimey, I wasn't aware that I had filled out a police statement or similar).

Finally, he suggested that if I really wanted a working-holiday visa, I should go back to England and apply there. To ensure I did this, he said he would inform all embassies in neighbouring countries of my rejection in Delhi. Anyway, he added, there was a 13-week waiting list for an interview – and the situation would be the same in London.

I think the real reason I did not get my visa was because the Australian embassy in Delhi could not be bothered to process my application. It was less work for them to send me elsewhere and, of course, the enormous cost to me was of no consequence. And surely if I was refused a visa on proper grounds, it would be a final and valid decision anywhere – so why was I practically told I could get one if I returned home?

When I reached London, I did get my visa, but in four hours, not 13 weeks. I also read a notice in the Australian embassy (in London) which confirmed that any persons under 25 years of age did not have to apply for an Australian working-holiday visa in their country of origin.

Now in Australia, I wonder if the Australian embassy staff in Delhi are enjoying what they obviously consider to be a working holiday as much as I am enjoying mine.

Charlotte Hindle – UK

We bought 1st-class tickets on the Gaya to Varanasi train. The train arrived and we got on. There was no 1st-class compartment, so we travelled in 2nd class. We reached Varanasi and and asked them to refund the difference.

We went to see the head ticket collector but he wasn't there. 'Ah' said a little man, 'You need the PA DEP SS' (person acting as deputy station supervisor, in case you're wondering). We found him but he sent us back to the head ticket collector who, this time, was there.

He said we had to have a certificate from the guard of the train saying there was no 1st class on that particular train. As the train was still at the station, of we went to find the guard. We found a new guard – the old one was in the rest room. When we went to the rest room, he wasn't there, however, the deputy station supervisor was there and he gave us the appropriate certificate.

We went back to find the head ticket collector but he was no longer there. We found him at the booking office. 'This certificate isn't from the guard.' he said. He went away and came back asking us to return to the booking office. We went to the wrong one but eventually found the right one. 'This certificate isn't from the guard.' we were told again. This man went away, but returned with the money.

The moral of the story is always get a certificate from the guard!

Lesley Reader

One old Indian cynic approached us in a bus station wanting to know why on earth we wanted to visit India. He said 'India has 800 million people, 800 million problems, and 800 million diseases' – there are times in India when it is difficult not to agree with him.

Charlotte Hindle – UK

If you intend to stay in India for a few months, you may wish to open a non-resident tourist bank account when you arrive.

You can do this at Grindlays Bank, 90 Mahatma Gandhi Rd, PO Box 141, Bombay 400 001.

A non-resident tourist account has to be funded with money from outside India. Indian rupees cannot be credited to this type of account.

Interest earned on non-resident tourist accounts is taxable at 30%. A non-resident tourist account has to be closed when you leave India (maximum of six months). The remaining balance will be paid back in foreign currency on producing your passport and confirmed onward air ticket.

There is another office in the UK at Minerva House, Montague Close, London SE1 9DH.

Two great Indian authors are R K Naragan, whose stories set in a fictitious South Indian town capture the character and atmosphere of India; and Mulk Raj Anand, whose novels give a good, unromantic view of Indian life, as well as an insight to what those rickshaw wallahs and street urchins are chatting about.

A brilliant book about Indian women is *Unveiling India* by Anees Jung.

D Berg & M Sells – Australia

The most sensible thing I did in India was to buy a 1st-class Indrail Pass. This saved me an enormous amount of hassle and it was extremely simple making train reservations in the larger cities. The only draw back is that you cannot purchase it inside India.

Michael Fredholm – Sweden

I learned two magic words for those inevitable times when things go wrong with your flight and no one else cares less – 'Duty Officer'. This is the only individual empowered to make decisions.

My flight from Agra to Bombay had been cancelled, I was expected by someone in Bombay, and wanted Indian Airlines to convey a message to them to let them know I was delayed and would be arriving on another flight, etc.

I handed my message to the clerk handling my reservations and he agreed to send it. For the next hour, I watched my message slowly disappear under a pile of 'papers to be attended to'.

Finally, I asked for the duty officer. He was pointed out to me, I explained my request, he told the clerk to send the message and it was done immediately.

Another time, Indian Airlines refused to rebook a ticket issued by Air India, and Air India refused to rebook the same ticket because the flight was on Indian Airlines. The duty officer remedied the situation. Also, whenever I needed a meal or hotel vouchers because of missed connections, it was only with the aid of the duty officer that they were issued.

David Bressoud – USA

We were lucky enough to obtain discount on air tickets from Quito, Ecuador to Delhi, via Paris. We paid US$1200 each. The catch was that we had to stay in Paris for seven days while we waited for our Indian visa to come through.

After going to the Indian embassy in Paris, we were told that we could not have the visas issued because we should have got them done in our own country before travelling. This would have been nine months ago, and the visas would have lost their validity by now.

We insisted that there must be another way to obtain an Indian visa and a decision was made to telex Canada for a clearance. Then a visa could be issued for C$50.

Every day we returned to the visa office in Paris to see Mr Bir, the man with all the authority. We ended up having to change our flight out of Paris three times in 15 days. The clearance from Canada had not been received.

On the 16th day, close to broke due to the high cost of everything in Paris, we went to see Mr Bir again (we had a flight out of France at 12 noon). Mr Bir's helper had seen us earlier, killing time at the metro. Perhaps he thought we had been sleeping in the subway? Anyway, we managed to get the visas without the clearance from Canada and away we went.

The authorities in Paris say it is mandatory that you get your visa in your own country before travelling. Obviously it is not. Mr Bir could have fixed the whole thing up in a day if he wasn't such an unsympathetic asshole.

Marie & Marc – Canada

We purchased a 30-day Indrail pass (UK£150) at the Indian Railways Sales Agent (tel (01) 9032411), SDEL 21 York House, Empire Way, Wembley HA9 0PA.

The agent will make advance reservations providing you do this at least 90 days ahead. If you can stick to your pre-planned travel arrangements this works well, as all you have to do in India is look up your name on the reservation listings at the station 30 minutes before the departure of your train.

You can change the advance reservations locally without any problems, but you do have to pay an Rs 10 administration charge for every change. All our train trips went without a hitch.

Guido Doyer – England

In reference to transferring money to India, I found it to be a simple process. My mother deposited UK£500 at Thomas Cook in Melbourne, Australia, and within 24 hours I picked up my travellers' cheques in Delhi. The staff were really nice and handed my money over quickly, all smiles.

Katherine Knox – Australia

New Delhi

The best budget hotel I found in the area of the Main Bazaar, opposite New Delhi station, is called the *Prince's Palace Guest House*. It was opened about six months ago and is clean with comfortable beds. The owner speaks very good English and is extremely helpful. A single room costs Rs 45.

R Lipsey – England

The best value food in Connaught Place has to be the Middle Eastern buffet at *El Arab*. The food is good and you can eat as much as you like.

After one month in India, the attraction of a real steak at the *Imperial* is overwhelming. It costs about Rs 55.

The *Hotel Kanishka* does an excellent buffet for Rs 80, but you have to dress respectably if you want the staff to treat you well.

George Porter – England

Himachal Pradesh
Manali

The *Meadows Hotel* has rooms with a supply of hot water for Rs 75. Good food is also available.

The Bookworm has a good selection of books in the English language, including two shelves of books relating to India. It is a library and costs Rs 5 to join, then Rs 1 for each book you borrow. The library is closed Sundays, but open every other day from 2.30 to 6 pm.

Joan Lindeman – Australia

Jammu & Kashmir
Srinigar

Butt's Clermont House Boats, north of the Hazratbal mosque, have wonderful food and great service. You can use canoes for free. No hawkers are allowed.

It costs around Rs 300 including all meals, tea, and fruit during season. Prices are negotiable off-season.

One of the most enjoyable things I've done in India is walk across the path dividing the lake at sunset.

Gary McMahon

I recommend *Houseboat Ceylon*, opposite Gate 2 on Dal Lake. I know it's hard to recommend individual houseboats, but I have stayed at this one several times over five years. It costs Rs 60 per person, and this includes excellent food. It's extremely comfortable, friendly and completely hassle free.

Liz Maudslay – England

Uttar Pradesh
Corbett National Park

Chilla is a fairly unknown corner of the park, which makes it nice to visit. Most of the animals you find in the rest of the park can be found in Chilla too.

We had a lovely evening at the *Tourist Bungalows* sipping tea and learning Hindi. There is one elephant available for rides in season. A bus goes from Hardwar to Chilla. Tell the bus driver to drop you off at the Tourist Bungalows.

Chloe Fiering – USA

Varanasi

Beware of aggressive dogs in this city. My travelling companion suffered an unprovoked attack by a group of 10 dogs, one of which bit my friend's thigh.

Getting shots for rabies in India is a major hassle. We eventually discovered that the government-run Kiburchaura Hospital gives shots for rabies free of charge, however, it's not the cleanest place so bring your own needles.

The hospital treats 200 people per day for animal bites (mainly dogs and monkeys). Unfortunately, 14 shots in the abdomen, one shot per day, is the only method of treatment in Varanasi. Not wanting to spend any more time in Varanasi, we obtained the name and address of a hospital in Calcutta and went there instead.

Once in Calcutta, we discovered that having injections at a government hospital involves endless red tape and queuing.

We became frustrated and turned to the US consulate for help. They put us on to the Pasteur Institute, in Calcutta, which sells rabies serum, if you have a letter of authorisation from your doctor.

My friend is still having injections at a private clinic near the US consulate. We learned that you can have six injections over a period of three months.

Jay Kinn – USA

West Bengal
Calcutta

The South-East Railway Booking Office is now sending all foreigners to a new office at 17 Fairlie Place. When we visited the office, however, it was not yet in use. We ended up buying our tickets at the Eastern Railway Booking Office at 6 Fairlie Place.

Jay Kinn – USA

Rajasthan
Jaisalmer

During my travels in Rajasthan, I found a clean restaurant called *Treat Restaurant* one flight up in a building opposite Salim Singh Havali.

The cuisine includes Chinese, Indian and Continental (I'd stick to Indian food) and you can ask for milder seasoning if you prefer.

Patrice Campbell – USA

Mt Abu

Mt Abu definitely deserves a plug as a great spot for foreigners who need a break from the real India. The children alone make it worthwhile. This is the first place I went where I wasn't continually assaulted by hordes of brats demanding baksheesh or screaming 'What's your name?' at me.

On the negative side, I thought I was beyond feeling anger at anything I saw, heard or encountered in India until I went to the Delwara temples. I stopped dead at the sign at the entrance which reads, 'Warning entry of ladies in monthly course is strictly prohibited any ladies in monthly course, if enters any of the temples she may suffer.'

This didn't apply to me but if it had, I'd have marched in without delay. After a brief struggle with my India-corroded moral code, I paid my Rs 5 and went in.

I'm curious to know whether any Jain women challenged the ban and, if so, what form the ensuing suffering took. Lathi blows from a policeman who sniffed out the dreaded secret? Divine wrath in a more subtle form – sterility forever?

Louise Hope – USA

Ranthambhor Park

As a park, this is quite picturesque and the tigers seem placid and are easy to spot. Accommodation is a problem. On arrival in Sawai Madopur, everything was organised through the local tourist office. The available accommodation in Sawai Madopur is appalling. For Rs 30, you need to hassle hard to get the sheets changed, electricity seems to be on the blink and, even with the fan working, sleeping is difficult during the hot season, or during the monsoon.

The cost of a jeep tour through the park costs Rs 200 and takes about four hours. You get picked up at 5.30 am, so a group of six people makes it fairly cheap.

The guide we had was excellent.
Greg Kempton – Australia

Bombay

The famous *Taj Mahal Hotel* in Colaba has an interesting history. It was built by a rich Indian who had travelled to England and discovered that London hotels often had signs in reception saying 'No Indian monkeys permitted'. He was so outraged at such blatant prejudice that on returning home he had the Taj Mahal Hotel built

and a sign placed in reception that read 'No British dogs permitted'.

While in England, he had commissioned a French architect to do the design and the plans were sent to India. When it was built, the French architect came to see his great work and found that it had been built back to front.

The beautiful front facade with Michelangelesque dome was facing away from the sea-front and was hidden, while the plainly designed back overlooked the 'Gateway to India' and the harbour. He was so upset that he committed suicide.

Charlotte Hindle – UK

Maharashtra
Pune

I spent seven weeks staying at the Rajneesh ashram. Bhagwan and his disciples are not too popular with the police and other authorities, so the ashram may be moving. The Bhagwan himself is rather frail and could die at any moment. I don't know what would happen to the ashram then.

When I was at the ashram (with about 5000 others), it cost around Rs 60 for three meals per day. The disciples no longer wear their *malas* (bead necklace with guru's photo), nor dress in any particular colour.

The emphasis within the ashram is on meditation, dynamic or any other kind. Tantric sexual rites did take place 10 years ago, but are certainly not organised now. In this age of AIDS, a much more responsible attitude to sex is strongly urged. You must have a recent certificate showing a negative result to an AIDS antibodies test in order to be able to participate in any of the courses now run by ashram therapists.

Many sightseers, both Indian and western, turn up at the ashram. The overall atmosphere is very soft and loving in a quiet and gentle way. The emphasis now is to look inside yourself, but this sort of thing doesn't find its way into the newspapers!

Kavido

The *Chinese Room Oriental*, Continental Chambers, Korue Rd, Pune 411004, has beautiful food. We paid Rs 18 for a great meal. They also do catering.

Michael Wallington – England

A one-day meditation course at the ashram costs Rs 10. You get delicious western-style vegetarian meals for Rs 20. There is an AIDS test restriction. Nothing is more aggravating (or costly) than being asked for your AIDS test certificate at the gate.

It costs Rs 300 to obtain the certificate from doctors in Bombay, and it's a four-hour train trip each way from Pune.

As Rajneesh is sick, there are additional restrictions – no strong perfumes or lotions, and no people with contagious ailments.

Otherwise, it's quite a colourful and interesting place with a variety of courses and activities. Rajneesh's discourses are often amusing.

Rahul Bedi – Canada

Goa
Colva Beach

I was wrapped in the restaurants on the beach at Colva. *Connie M* was my favourite as it was cheap, and had great food and drinks. *Lactancica Restaurant* also organises a bus to the Anjuna market on Wednesdays, departing at 10 am. The trip takes about two hours and costs Rs 30.

The Anjuna market is still an amazing scene. I noticed a lot of hippies there doing some business to support their life styles. I preferred to do my bargaining with the Indians. The hippies started at ridiculously inflated prices and would not accept reasonable offers.

Paul Boers – Australia

Andhra Pradesh
Hyderabad

The *Hyd-Inn* is great if you like filthy sheets, bed bugs, bells ringing outside your window at 6 am, people screaming in the corridors, hideous cooking smells, a turd on your bathroom floor and pigeons in the air-conditioner.

The tourist office is fantastic and has pamphlets for everything.

D Berg & M Sells – Australia

Kerala
Ponmudi

Ponmudi is a hill station in west Kerala. It's a beautiful place, not touristy, and very primitive. You get there by bus from the central bus station of Trivandrum and it takes three and a half hours. There are a few buses each day. The narrow road leading to the village passes through beautiful, wild forest with cool air.

The villagers are not used to seeing European people. There is a small market every day from 4 to 5 pm. A small factory for drying and packing tea leaves is at end of the only street. Almost all the people in the village work on tea plantations.

Above the village, there is a *Government Tourist Complex* – a peaceful place with a good restaurant. The rooms cost Rs 48 and are nice and clean.

Above the government tourist complex, there is a road leading to the top of the mountain. It takes 20 minutes to walk up and, at the top, there is a marvellous view.

Iddo Morag – Israel

Madras

The bus from the Indian Airlines office to the airport costs Rs 20 per person. Auto-rickshaws will pick you up from your hotel and take you to the airport, at a prearranged time and price, for the same price.

Paul Cusack – Australia

Tamil Nadu
Chidambaram

In front of the Hotel Tamil Nadu, there is the incredible and fantastic *Milky Mist* where you can buy the best sweets in India.

J Ollé & S Oliver – Spain

NEPAL

The road from Tibet

I took a four-day trip by Chinese bus to the Nepal border. The Chinese buses are definitely less reliable than the Japanese ones, so people travelling on a tight schedule should avoid these. There is a big price difference – Y120 (FEC) for the Chinese bus, and Y260 (FEC) for the Japanese bus.

Like in all Chinese buses, your legs will probably be cramped and stiff unless you get a good seat.

The bus is slow to climb, so the 210 km to Gyantse takes about 10 hours. Two of the passes are higher than 5000 metres. Because the monastery is closed in the afternoons, you are not able to visit the famous Pango chorten. (Some Dalai Lama pictures and some group pressure may persuade someone to open the Chorten even late in the evening.)

In Sakya, there is a new hotel, run by Tibetans, with at least 20 dormitories each containing four beds. Many roadworkers and housebuilders stay in these dormitories. Beds costs Y5 RMB. There are roosters, hens and dogs all over the place.

The monks in Sakya are after money. Make sure you get a ticket or they'll let you pay twice. People with cameras are followed until they take a photograph, then they are charged a fine of Y20 RMB. Pilgrims donating less than Y2 to the local lama did not receive his blessings.

Tingri West is a beautiful place to stay with superb views of the

Himalayas. There are three hostels there with a total of 25 beds.

We drove 70 km further to a Chinese army post. You can sleep there but it's a big rip-off. Although they have some six-bed dorms, we had to pay Y10 FEC each to sleep with 20 other people on the ground. The soldiers put some blankets down on the stone floor. There is one tap (cold water) and two big kettles for boiling hot water. The soldiers simply push you aside when they want water.

Another group of travellers had to pay Y50 FEC each because one of the soldiers insisted a blanket was missing in the morning. No one could hide a blanket in their pack, but the Chinese officials refused to check. They just wanted the money.

In the morning, when the buses continue their journey to Nepal, the washing facilities are still locked.

On the plus side, it's interesting to watch the soldiers 'disco-dancing' to music from a cassette player in the evening. They like to dance with foreigners and have special dances, like 'bumping'.

From here, you go from a height of 5220 metres to 1200 metres within a couple of hours. Because of the landslides near Zhangmu, and the fact that Friendship Bridge is still closed to cars, you have to walk down a steep hill for three to four hours.

You can hire porters to carry your bags to the Chinese border for Y2 to Y3 per hour. From the Chinese side of the border to the Nepalese side, rates are Rs 25 for a porter.

If you want to change RMB to rupees at the bank, you have to prove that you originally changed some currency into RMB at the official rate. The black market rate, in Zhengmu, is Rs 6 to Y1 FEC, Rs 4 to Y1 RMB.

Taxis from the Nepalese border to Kathmandu cost around Rs 100 per person. A maximum of four people can fit in one taxi. On our arrival day, there were so many tourists that we could not bargain to pay less than Rs 150 each.

Wouter Tiems – Netherlands

Nepal has just recently changed its policy making it very expensive to bring in a bike from India. The first

Nepali Demon Mask

seven days are free, then it costs Rs 100 for the next 30 days, Rs 200 for the second lot of 30 days, and Rs 300 for the third lot of 30 days. This rule only applies to Indian vehicles, not cycles brought over from Europe.

Bartholomew's Indian subcontinent map isn't nearly detailed enough. The TT maps road atlas is quite good and available everywhere.

Robert Lebovic – USA

Kathmandu

You describe the Bir Hospital in Kathmandu as modern. The building might be a few years old but conditions are appalling, infection is rife and no drugs are kept on the premises.

Having worked at the Bir Hospital, we recommend the new United Mission Hospital in Patan instead. It is an excellent hospital and charges are minimal.

Helen Wright – England

We went trekking in Nepal and found that every man and his dog were applying for an Indian visa after the trek. The normal procedure is one day lining up for the form, another day handing it in with passport and rupees, then two more days for processing.

After much hassle getting a form, we were informed that they would accept the applications in seven days time and then take two days to process them. Ten days in Kathmandu isn't much fun when you've already completed any treks that could fill in the time.

The way around the problem is to buy a flight to India (eg Kathmandu to Varanasi, US$54) on Indian Airlines. This will force them to hurry things up.

John Garlick – New Zealand

In Kathmandu, extending visas for up to 30 days is easy and free.

While in Kathmandu, I needed medical care and found the Patan Hospital to be excellent. If you need treatment, it's best to come reasonably early in the morning as the hospital staff cannot deal with too many patients in one day.

I financed my week-long stay in Nepal with the winnings from my visit to Casino Nepal in the *Hotel Soalte Oberoi*. I read that they provided free coupons in return for used airline tickets, and it's true!

Michael Fredholm – Nepal

PAKISTAN

The dates given by travel agents as being suitable for travelling on the Karakoram Highway are related to the fact that on those days, there will be no dynamite used in road construction. The dates are 1, 2, 3, 15, 17, 18, of each month.

Wouter Tiems – Netherlands

The road from Iran

The sealed road ends at the Iranian exit gate as you roll into Taftan. Immediately, you notice the squalor and flies.

Taftan itself is a dirty border town with shacks and filth everywhere.

The government in Pakistan exercises less control over its people than the government in Iran, and locals stroll back and forth across the border.

It's easy to change money outside banking times although rates aren't particularly good.

G Anderson & K Wells – USA

The road from India

The Hyderbad-Barmer rail link is still closed. Crossing by rail from Lahore involves a change of trains at Amritsar.

There have been killings in this city every day for the last few weeks, some quite random.

The word from friends in Pakistan is that foreigners are preferred targets as they make bigger headlines and demonstrate the governments lack of control.

The train also stops in two other large Sikh towns where attacks are a possibility. Since Indian bus and train stations have never been known for their safety, it might be an idea to give the overland trail a miss. Flights cost Rs 350 from Lahore to Delhi.

Robert Churchill – USA

Gilgit

Travellers running out of film should go to the *Serena Lodge*, five km north of Gilgit. Films are stored in a cool place, which cannot be said of the sometimes steaming hot bazaar shops.

Wouter Tiems – Netherlands

Sust

Immediately after your arrival, go to the Nadco bus office to reserve places for the bus of next morning. There is busy constructing going on. The best and biggest hotel, the *Khunjarab Hotel*, has about 20 rooms and costs Rp 150 per person. The second largest hotel is German and has three dormitories each with 12 beds. It costs Rp 20 per person.

Six km out of Sust, four km past the bridge, in the direction of the Khunjerab Pass, are some hot springs. The springs are signposted by a heap of stones. A little Suzuki bemo will take you there for Rp 30. The springs are surrounded by a stone wall, so you can have a great bath.

Wouter Tiems – Netherlands

SRI LANKA

Because of the war, it's a great time for the tourist (not the locals) to be in Sri Lanka. The number of tourists has decreased from 407,000 in 1982 to 230,000 in 1986 to an estimated 100,000 in 1987.

I found that tourists were unaffected by the war, even in the ancient cities. I didn't go to the east coast. Military presence was less apparent than in northern India.

There is no need to object to the two-fare system. Equivalent attractions would cost as much or more in the west and, lets face it, even the poorest budget traveller is quite wealthy in Sri Lanka. All visitors to

Sri Lanka are enjoying themselves. We can't do much about the poverty of the people there, but the money we spend would help a little. The common attitude of travellers is that things should be as close to free as possible, and this is disgusting.

Gary McMahon

Ancient Cities

The *Tissawewa Rest House* at Anuradhapura is superb. Admission charges are now Rs 120 for each prime spot or Rs 360 for admission to all four.

The Mirisavatiya Dagoba is now split into four pieces so you can see the bricks. You are not allowed to take photographs.

It's a bit of an ordeal getting to Medirigiriya, however, it's worth it for the setting in the jungle and paddy fields. Also, it's likely that you'll be the only one there. All four buddhas are in good condition.

The *Sigiriya Rest House* is quite good. There is a nice lotus pond, interesting excavations, and pleasant grounds.

Gary McMahon

Colombo

I stayed at the *Palm Beach Hotel*, on Saram Rd, Mount Lavina, for Rs 250. The rooms are large and spotless, some of them have balconies. You can use the swimming pool and the beach is only two minutes walk away. The food is good and there's a bar.

A beer or cup of tea at sunset on the terrace of the Mount Lavina Hotel is one of life's great pleasures.

Changing rupees back into dollars is completely hassle free. I had even lost my currency declaration form. A good way to obtain dollars to use in the duty free shops is to cash too many travellers' cheques. The Bank of Ceylon currency exchange on York St is one of the most quick and efficient I've used anywhere.

Gary McMahon

Kandy

I stayed in the private home of Mrs Sriya Devasunders, 40 Sangamitta Mawata, just past Jingle Bells. Rooms cost between Rs 50 to Rs 100. The food is great.

Gary McMahon

1987 was not a happy year for Sri Lanka. Even after the signing of the Peace Accord, there was still fierce fighting in the North and the East. Opposition to the Accord has turned to violence, with incidents reported all over the south. However, as long as one is sensible and careful, there is little danger to the visitor. (The CTB bus drivers are probably more life threatening.)

Sri Lanka is still a beautiful country – where else can you travel from an empty beach to an ancient city to a country tea estate, in a matter of hours?

Personal Safety

In July 1987, JR Jayewardene and Rajiv Gandhi signed a Peace Accord to stop the fighting in the north and east of Sri Lanka. Even though the immediate response in the south was violence, there was a real feeling of hope that this might have stopped the war. People were travelling to the north and east of Sri Lanka and the Indian Peace Keeping Force (IPKF) was welcomed as liberator. This did not last long. The fighting resurged with a vengeance and refugees fled from the north and east of the country. There is no indication that the fighting will cease in the near future.

The opposition to the Accord in the south of Sri Lanka burst out in a blaze of violence with government buildings, buses and railway lines being destroyed and burned. The JVP, an extremist Sinhala party, launched a campaign of violence against the government in which over 70 officials were killed, including the Chairman of the ruling party. In retaliation, a pro-government group (The Green Tigers) has been formed which has been involved in various killings.

Officially, you can travel anywhere on the island, though it would be very stupid to travel anywhere north of Anuradhapura or east of an imaginary line between Polonnaruwa and Yala. Even Arugam Bay, which people were visiting last year, is now off-limits.

The violence in the south is very specific and there are not really any 'no-go' areas – be careful around Embilipitiya and Kataragama. Several large bombs exploded last year. Though difficult, you should try to avoid large crowds. The Pettah bus stand, in Colombo, was bombed twice.

The general mood of the country is tense and people are not as willing to discuss politics as they used to be. There have been reports of tourists being mugged and raped. Sri Lankans have a low opinion of western women, which is not helped by some tourists. Women should be covered from shoulders to knees – anything less is unacceptable.

Health

Last year, there was a serious outbreak of Japanese encephalitis resulting in over 100 deaths. You should be inoculated for your own protection. Chilaw and Anuradhapura were the worst affected areas. The risk of contracting malaria is increasing, so propylactics are essential.

Beaches

Hikkaduwa is still the loveliest beach and many people say that no one is hassled there. Unawatuna is very pretty and the UBR disco, held on Saturday nights, can be a lot of fun. The disco is a new venue – the old one fell down. Mirissa, west of Matara, on the south coast, is the prettiest and quietest beach bus has very little choice of accommodation and food.

Ancient Sites
There are now many wonderful sites which are very much off the beaten track. If you have time, try to get to Buduruvagala, near Wellawaya; Munnarwaram, near Chilaw; Nalanda, near Dambulla; and Yapahuwa, near Maho and Panduvasnavara.
Places to Stay
Availability of rooms in hotels is hardly ever a problem in Sri Lanka and accommodation prices have remained stable.
Places to eat
In Colombo, the price of food in the market is rising alarmingly but the restaurants have not put their prices up. The Seafood Restaurant, behind the Regal Cinema, and the Little Tree Restaurant, next to the Regal Cinema, both do good rice and curries for less than Rs 40. The Wimpy Corner, Galle Rd, Bambalapitiya, sells good western food for under Rs 40. The Shanti Vihar, corner of Bullers Rd and Havelock Rd, makes very good, cheap South Indian food.
In Kandy, the Flower Song, opposite the YMCA is an excellent Chinese restaurant where you can eat for less than Rs 60 per head. You can get nice soya ice-cream at the Soya Centre in the YMCA.
Getting Around
Even though a lot of CTB buses were burned and railway lines pulled up last July, the transport around the island has not been affected much. Transport is still very cheap, frequent and uncomfortable. There have been complaints published in newspapers regarding tourists bribing railway officials to get seats. You can always get a seat if you go to the station the night before you intend to leave.

TURKEY

The bus system is impressive. The best of many bus services is AYDIN. These buses stop regularly and are washed down each time. Free tea is provided at each stop, and a free breakfast is provided on overnight trips.

Chocolates and bottled water are available all the time and the stewards, instead of going to sleep on the back window ledge, are continually sweeping the central aisle or splashing passengers with eau-de-cologne. It's also cheap.

A student card gets you 60% discount on all flights and they can be bought quite easily. I got one showing an out-of-date student library card and then, bargaining for flights at a travel agency, discovered that any student card bought in Turkey is invalid within that country (but quite valid outside Turkey). The reason for the card being invalid in Turkey itself is because they are often obtained illegally here by foreigners and especially by large numbers of Iranians.

Charlotte Hindle – UK

Bursa

Özyurt Ögrenci Yurdu, Maksem Caddesi 46, is a nice, cheap pension where you can get a bed from A$1 to A$5. There are four-bed rooms with lockers, constant hot water, a library and games room. You can change money at the pension.

Istanbul

Hors Seda (tel 5211844), Ordekli Bakal Sok No 1/2, Kumkapi, is a small, family-run seafood restaurant. It is within walking distance of Sultanahmet where most travellers stay and is one hundred times better than the nearby tourist restaurants serving food cooked eight hours ago. At Hors Seda, the dishes are fresh, delicious and cheap. All the locals eat there ... need I say more?

Charlotte Hindle – UK

Tom Brosnahan, the author of Turkey – a travel survival kit, made these notes while researching the latest edition of the guide.

Lots of people seem to have discovered that Turkey today is like Greece was in the good old days – beautiful, friendly, peaceful and cheap.

Istanbul, Troy, Cappadocia, and the Aegean and Mediterranean beach resorts are all very busy in summer. To avoid the crowds, go from late April through mid-June, or late September through November. The most interesting coastal villages are Assos (Behramkale) in the North Aegean; Datca, near Marmaris; Patara and Kalakan, east of Fethiye, on the Mediterranean coast. The most popular area for shoestring travellers is east Turkey with its wide open spaces, extensive history, friendly people, few crowds and very low prices. The major bonuses are the trek up Nemrut Dagi to view the temples, Sanhurfa for its wonderful old bazaar, Dogubeyazit for the majestic Agri Dagi and Ishak Pasha's Palace, and Van for its kilim dealers.

For less touristy pleasures, Gaziantep abounds in cheap pistachio nuts, Malatya is awash in delicious apricots, Antakya is half- Turkish and half-Arabic in culture, and Erzurum boasts magnificent Seljuk Turkish architecture.

There is a well-defined 2000-km route through the east that can be done in two weeks or so by bus. Hotel prices at the bottom end of the scale range from US$1 to US$3 per person, meals are delicious and can cost as little as US$2.

The high plateau (Erzurum, Kars, Dogubeyazit, Nemrut) is very cold and windy except from June through September. The south- east

(Diyarbakir, Sanhurfa, Gaziantep, Antakya) is blazing hot and dry in July and August.

In August, it's best to travel from north (Trabzon) to south. In May, it's best to travel in the opposite direction – head north from Cappadocia or Adana.

When travelling from north to south, follow the fertile Black Sea coast to Trabzon or Hopa, then move inland to Kars and Erzurum; east to Dogubeyazit; west to Diyarbakir; west to Agri, then south to Lake Van's eastern shore. From the city of Van, head west to Diyarbakir, then to Adiyaman or Malatya for the trek up Nemrut Dagi. Once the weather is a bit cooler, head south to Sanhurfa, Gaziantep and Antakya. Starting from the south, head for Antakya, Gaziantep and Sanhurfa first before it gets too hot, then head up on the plateau to the other places.

If you've got extra time, go deep into the mountains southeast of Sivas to Divrigi, a pretty village set in a fertile dead-end valley. Above the town are a medieval fortress and a grandiose Seljuk Great Mosque and hospital. Come out of Divrigi to Sivas, where there are many more good Seljuk building, no tourists and lots of convenient transport.

Tom Brosnahan

. . . . NOTES . . . .

India

Agra The *Hotel Lauries* is brilliant value. A huge room with attached bathroom costs Rs 100.

Bombay *Dippy's Juice Bar* makes great fruit drinks, if you can stand the junkies who hang out there all night long!

Cochin Antique lovers may be interested to know that there are three good shops near the Jewish synagogue. Dowry boxes, unique to the state of Kerala, can be bought for about Rs 900.

Jaisalmer The best place to eat at is the *Jain Restaurant*, 150 metres before you reach the State Bank of Bikaner. They have large pots of food cooking on gas burners outside the restaurant itself.

Mysore The *Shanghai Restaurant*, unlike most Chinese places in India, has delicious, authentic meals for around Rs 30.

Udaipur The *Padmini Hotel Palace*, 27 Gulab Bagh Rd, costs US$8 to US$10 for a double room.

The *Hotel Swagat*, 29 City Station Rd, near Surajpole Choraya, costs US$4 to US$5 for a double room

Nepal

Kathmandu The *Tibet Guest House* is in the Thamel area, near the Pheasant Lodge. It's clean and costs Rs 100 per night.

The *Tara Guest House* in Thamel is clean, safe and reasonably priced.

Lufthansa now flies direct from Europe to Kathmandu.

Nagarkot *Mount Everest Lodge* is clean and costs Rs 15 to Rs 25 per night.

Pokhara The *Butterfly Lodge*, Lake Side, Baidam, Ward No 6, is very clean, quiet and close to the lake.

MIDDLE EAST

IRAN

We travelled through Iran with eight others on an organised London to Delhi trip. Originally, 16 people intended to travel but, due to visa hassles, only half of us made it!

Getting a visa for Iran was difficult. The London embassy informed us that it was impossible for British people to obtain an Iranian visa and that it would take six weeks for Australians.

In the end, we went to Ireland and waited three days for a personal interview at the Iranian embassy there. We were successful.

It's virtually compulsory for women applying for visas to wear headscarves. Women won't be considered at all if unaccompanied by a male traveller. One female in our group was rejected on sight due to her appearance. The Iranians place heavy importance on ultra-conservative dress, even at the embassies. Even the visa photographs you submit are scrutinised.

Visas issued to our group members varied in length from seven to 10 days. If you happen to hold a Turkish passport you can visit Iran for 14 days without a visa.

During the rather long entry procedure, a member of our group accidentally tore up the wrong form and had a hell of a time explaining his way around the destruction of a state document. Eventually, some bright spark came to the rescue with clear sticky tape. Our friend now has a deep respect of official forms and never again wants to be given the opportunity to learn farsi for free.

The whole entry process lasted 24 hours. Fortunately, only the bus was impounded for all this time, and we were allowed to spend the night in a hotel 15 km down the road.

The border searches of our gear and of the bus were very thorough. Other groups passing through the Turkish/Iranian border at Gazargan reported the random removal of vehicle panels and laborious searches of travellers' possessions.

While sitting on the bus reading, a 'morals' inspector whizzed on to our bus and inspected the titles and cover pictures of our books. No sordid stuff allowed into Iran!

Some groups have recently been made to exchange US$150 per person at the official exchange rate. In other cases, only half the people on the bus were made to exchange this amount of money. We were lucky and didn't have to exchange anything.

Iran is very cheap if you use black market money. The best rates we managed to get were 800 rials for US$1 and 1000 rials for UK£1 (compared to the official rate of approximately 68 rials to US$1).

Just inside Iran, moneychangers operate openly at the exit from the customs compound. We found out from locals that these fellows are rounded up at irregular intervals, their money confiscated.

The day we arrived at the border, Isfahan had been bombed and we were not allowed to go there. An escort is supposed to accompany each vehicle. Our bus ended up with an unpleasant specimen as an escort. Another group travelling through at the same time had a really nice escort who let them to stay at his relative's place overnight and gave them a bit of a guided tour.

With black market money, accommodation is very cheap. For example, the *Hotel International* in Tabriz worked out to cost less than US$5 each.

Women must be completely covered up, hiding hair, arms, feet and legs. Men must wear shirts with long sleeves – great in the hot weather. The situation is very strict around Tehran and less strict south of Yazd.

Food is boring and many shops have closed because of the war. Food shortages are common. All you get is kebabs and rice, occasionally chicken stew, tea and the odd soft drink.

Fuel is very cheap at 60 rials per litre for super and 4 rials per litre for diesel.

G Anderson & K Wells – USA

JORDAN

Attempts to secure a Jordanian visa in Egypt were thwarted by an Islamic holiday – the embassy was closed for a week. Scowl. Next I learned that the Jordanian embassy required a letter of introduction from my own embassy. Snarl. This problem is encountered at all embassies in Cairo. First we needed passports, then visas, and now letters of introduction. Bah!

For E£20, the British embassy will type a letter for you. I applied for my visa at 9 am and obtained it at 11.30 am, after coughing up a further E£60. On arrival at Aqaba (Jordan), I learned that visas are issued on the spot. Sigh.

R McLean – Wales

Petra

The Al Khalil Tea House, now called *Musa Spring Hotel*, has been extended and has five bedrooms. All facilities are kept exceptionally clean and the people running the place are very welcoming.

The cooking is occasionally done by one of the chefs from the Petra Forum Hotel. You can drink tea anytime and shower for free. It costs JD1.5 per person.

Minibuses to Aqaba and Amman stop right outside very early in the mornings.

Ian Brown – England

AUSTRALASIA

AUSTRALIA

Most European banks are part of the Eurocheque scheme, which enables customers to cash cheques in foreign countries. Many banks in Australia are also in the Eurocheque scheme, although they do not advertise the fact.

Westpac will cash Eurocheques worth up to UK£50 and charge A$2 commission. The National Bank Australia will cash Eurocheques worth up to UK£100, but charge A$5 commission (per cheque). ANZ banks sometimes refuse to cash them, however, if they do accept these cheques, they won't charge any commission. The Commonwealth Bank will cash Eurocheques worth up to UK£100 and do not charge any commission.

Denis Crampton – England

Prices for secondhand vehicles are lower in Australia than in the US or Britain.

I bought a 1972 Ford Escort panel van in Brisbane for A$999. The manager of Barry Parade Motors in Brisbane was thinking of running a scheme aimed at long-stay tourists, whereby he'd guarantee to buy a vehicle back when the purchaser was leaving, for a prearranged price.

Such an arrangement would remove one of the major worries attached to buying a car on holiday. He bought my car back for A$350 which was pretty generous considering the state it was in.

Denis Crampton – England

New South Wales
Katoomba

The *Katoomba Mountain Lodge* (tel (047) 823933), 31 Lurline St, has dorm beds for A$7 each. The dormitories are open all day and there are no curfews. There are also rooms from A$14 per person, A$18 for bed and breakfast.

The lodge is a one minute walk to Katoomba shopping centre and five minutes walk from the Katoomba railway station.

Garry Blanchard

Sydney

The *Lamrock Hostel* is a one minute walk from the beach. It has large, clean rooms, some with private bathrooms. Rooms costs A$15 per person in a dormitory and A$20 for a double room. You can hire linen and blankets for A$5 for the duration of your stay.

The hostel has kitchen and laundry facilities and a reading room, which is very popular. You can hire Mini Mokes for day trips.

V Vedik – Australia

If you want to eat at a non-smoking restaurant, there's *Eve's Harvest Vegetarian Restaurant* at Rozelle, and the *Wei Song* at Bondi and Neutral Bay. The *Moustache Restaurant* at Crows Nest has a separate room for smokers.

Bed and Breakfast Sydneyside has a registry of family homes that can provide the visitor with a private room and a bed for the night. There are homes in some of the nicest parts of Sydney, with facilities ranging from basic to luxurious.

Single accommodation costs A$30 to A$50 per night and doubles range from A$45 to A$80. The host families can provide guests with information about Sydney.

For more information, write to Alison Duncan, Bed and Breakfast Sydneyside, PO Box 555, Turramurra, NSW 2074, or ring (02) 4494430.

The new *Glebe Point Youth Hostel* is very pleasant, and a nice alternative to staying in Kings Cross. The rooms are clean and comfortable. The bedrooms are separated from the noisy communal area.

Megan O'Donnell – USA

I rode a bicycle from Sydney to Melbourne and parts of the trip were very hilly. If you travel along the coast from Sydney to Wollongong, you avoid many hills.

In Nowra, the Shoalhaven River is great for swimming and the ground near the golf course is good for camping, as is the golf course itself (but watch out, some golfers start very early in the morning).

At Ulla Dulla, halfway up the hill on the south side of town (but still in town and on the main road), there's a sign saying 'guest house'. The guest house is run by a woman named Flora, and costs A$15 for a single room. Showers, parking and breakfast is available. You can also use the fridge.

South of Bateman's Bay, there are plenty of beaches. From Cobargo to Brogo, it's extremely hilly though very pretty. In Eden, the *Australian Hotel* is a pub which sells Chinese takeaway. Rooms cost A$20 for a single and A$30 for a double. The bakery across the road is really good.

Around the side of the Australian Hotel, there is a small shopping arcade in which you'll find a national parks and wildlife information centre.

Heading south from Eden, just north of the Victorian border, there is a rest area with a water tank, to the side of the road. Genoa is the first town you reach in Victoria, and there's a caravan park just north of the Genoa River. At Cann River, the Aboriginal Craft Museum has a caravan park out the back which costs A\$12 per person.

In Orbost, hotels have single rooms for A\$15, but the grounds of the post office, churches and schools would be good for camping. In Lakes Entrance, there are some good unused farm buildings you can sleep in and this was the most beautiful area I rode through.

Warragul is one of the last stops along the Princes Highway before Melbourne and it's a great place with friendly people. Eastwards from Warragul, there are some really nice churches to see, especially one Catholic church in Bairnsdale which shows some demons dragging damned souls off to hell.

From Bairnsdale to Melbourne, the land is very flat, a cyclists dream. Watch out for Sundays and public holidays. In small towns it can be difficult to find somewhere selling food.

Good places to stay in all country towns include abandoned houses; under the roofs of post offices (where the post boxes are kept); in churches (one door is usually left unlocked); or you can just meet people and stay with them.

For showers, if you can't find a caravan park with freebies, don't forget swimming pools, some service stations, and you could always ask someone – people are very friendly.

Dandenong is the last major town before reaching Melbourne. Opposite the railway station, across the park, is a large church. You can sleep on ground sheets under the eaves of this church.

Mark Donahue – Australia

Port Macquarie

Lindel Traveller's Hostel, 5 Hindman St, has excellent facilities and is very clean. There is a roomy kitchen and a television room that guests can use.

Northern Territory
Ayers Rock

The campground costs A\$6 per person and there are restaurants and a supermarket 400 metres away. Food and most other things are about twice the price that they are in Alice Springs.

Sarah Collins

There is a guided walk along the base of Ayers Rock, covering the history, geology and mythology of the rock. It starts from the foot of the tourist climb each morning at 10 am, takes about 30 minutes, and is well worthwhile.

The one not to miss is the Liru walk during which two aborigines describe and demonstrate weapon-making, tool-making, food-gathering and fire-making. It was utterly fascinating.

It is only run three times a week, Tuesdays, Thursdays and Saturdays. It's always full and booking is essential.

Denis Crampton – England

Coburg Peninsula

If travelling by four-wheel drive, in the dry season only around here, it's interesting to drive through Arnhem Land, to the peninsular fence line. The fence holds back Bantang cattle, water buffalo, deer and other animals. There is some excellent flora on the way. The track is good for most of the way, with about one hour of rough terrain after the turn off from Murginella.

The camping ground at Smith Point only has one shower and toilet. There is a small store which opens for a couple of hours each day. The camping area is well-shaded, 100 metres from the beach, with a cool breeze most of the time. For camping and tourist permits, write to the Conservation Commission, Darwin, Northern Territory.

Try to travel early in the morning or later in the evening – mid-afternoon is not a good time.

Bring enough fuel with you to last through your return trip. From Jabiru, it takes about six to eight hours driving time one way. When I was last up there, fuel cost 90 cents a litre.

The area is usually booked out from May to July, so book ahead. We paid A$20 per week to camp. The conservation people are nice and will process your permits within a working week.

Darwin

Backpacker's International, 88 Mitchell St, is particularly friendly. A positive atmosphere prevailed, created to a great extent by the energetic staff.

Ivan, the owner, was frequently willing and eager to take travellers on various tours and trips.

We were also impressed with the frequent barbecues, the outdoor pool and the access to the two kitchens.

The hostel is relatively small, but it's great for meeting people from all over the world.

Karen Podolchak – Canada

Queensland
Cairns

Crocodylus Village (tel (070) 536690) is right in the rainforest, about 130 km north of Cairns. The minimum number of trees has been cut down to make way for the buildings, so the natural environment is preserved.

Accommodation is basic, dorm beds cost A$9, self-contained units (for up to eight people) cost A$40. There are cooking facilities, a restaurant, a swimming pool and a laundry. A courtesy bus will run you to the nearest beach, Cow Bay, which is a few km away. You can also make arrangements to visit a nearby island.

You can book to stay at Crocodylus at any Cairns YHA hostel. There is a public bus (A$28 return) which departs from Cairns. The address is

Crocodylus Village, Buchanan Creek Rd, Cow Bay, North Queensland.

A Swedish traveller had gems and money stolen from his moneybelt left in the safe at *Parkview Hostel*, 174-178 Grafton St, Cairns. Apparently, the safe not been opened by force, yet no one was able to offer him a satisfactory explanation as to how the theft could have occurred. Management told the traveller to go to his insurance company.

Inn the Tropics, Sheridan St, is great middle-range accommodation. It costs A$30 for two people, and you share a kitchen and bathroom.

Pro-dive still runs good dive courses which are well-organised, professional and excellent value.
Barnacle Bills, on the Esplanade, is a bustling, seafood restaurant, great for a slap-up treat.
J & E Dugdale – England

There's a big range of scuba courses around Cairns costing from A$180 to A$300. They last four or five days and include practical dives.
Go on the most expensive course you can afford as generally the more expensive courses are also more enjoyable (dives are often done on the outer reefs).
The Green Possum Bookshop, 55 Grafton St, has an interesting selection of books, pamphlets, T-shirts and posters.
The Underwater Camera Shop, Shop A10 in Traveltown, 21 Lake St,

Cairns, hires out underwater cameras and strobes. The same people run the Barrier Reef School of Underwater Photography and are very willing to offer advice on how to take good photographs under water.
Denis Crampton – England

Seafood A Go Go, on the corner of the Esplanade and Alpin St, is great for fresh fish (grilled, crumbed or in batter) and chips. The fish curry, seafood lasagne, and prawns are also recommended. Meals are served with salad, chips and/or rice and prices start at A$3.50. This restaurant is also a good meeting place for travellers.
Lisa Will – Australia

Great Barrier Reef

When I die I want to go to the Great Barrier Reef, one of the world's great wonders. Fortunately, there is a fair choice of day-trips from Cairns to the reef and islands. The cheaper trips include Fitzroy Island, A$14 with Hayles; Green Island, A$14 with Hayles or on the *Big Cat*; Michaelmas Cay and Hastings Reef, A$30 on the *Seastar II*; Moore Reef, A$35 with Hayles; and the Low Islands, A$40 from Port Douglas on the *Big Cat*.
While I was there, the Hayles people were handing out vouchers on all their boats entitling people to 10% off ferry tickets. Thus, by using Hayles to get to Green Island or Fitzroy Island, you would qualify for 10% off the Moore Reef ticket (worth having to say the least!).

The best coral I saw was on Hastings Reef, and Green Island had the widest range of fish.

Denis Crampton – England

Magnetic Island

Magnetic Island is eight km east of Townsville. A 20-minute ferry ride will take you to the island. Cars can be taken across on the vehicle ferry. *Foresthaven* (tel (077) 785153) is a budget resort for backpackers and families. It is next to the national park, close to shops and a public swimming pool. Plans for a swimming pool at Foresthaven itself are underway.

Perth Australia

Dinosaur – In these days of Levis and leisure suits a last authentic digger hat, with dangling corks to keep away the flies.

Dormitory beds cost A\$7 per night, double rooms from A\$25 per night. There is a restaurant at Foresthaven, but you can cook your own food in the communal kitchen if you prefer. A courtesy bus will take you to Picnic Bay and Arcadia Bay.

Townsville

The Great Barrier Reef Wonderland and the Sheraton Casino are now operational. Both are proving to be a major attraction for backpackers as well as other tourists.

With the opening of the Breakwater Marina, next to the casino, Townsville is becoming a stopping-off port for ocean-going yachts. Fast tourist boats leave the Marina and Wonderland (on Ross Creek) daily for the Great Barrier Reef and Palm Islands.

The Palm Islands are of great natural beauty and day trippers can, amongst other things, snorkel over coral and inspect the giant clam farm run by James Cook University.

Through the work of researchers at James Cook University and the Australian Institute of Marine Science, Townsville has become a major world centre for tropical marine studies. Both the university and the institute welcome visitors.

Globetrotters is the only hostel in Townsville to be constructed as a backpacker's hostel. The modern, tropical-style building was completed early this year and came into operation just before Easter.

M & M Dixon – Australia

Whitsunday Islands

Water taxis out to the Whitsundays are a ludicrous price – A$400 to Border Island! It's possible to fly by plane for about A$320.

The only islands accessible for camping are Whitsunday, Hook and the Molles Islands. The procedure is to book a place on a boat, then go to the Queensland National Parks and Wildlife ranger station near Shute Harbour and get the camping permit.

The national parks people have strict instructions not to give any advice to potential campers about what boats go where, or how much anything costs. I think this could be because locals are opposed to camping on the islands and the national parks association doesn't want to stir up trouble.

Stonehaven Beach on Hook Island can be reached on the trimaran *Tingara* for A$35 return. A boat to North Molle Island costs A$28 return and a boat to the Whitsundays costs A$30 to A$45, depending on which beach you want to go to.

The car park at Airlie Beach is free and there are no restrictions on overnight parking which makes it popular with the camper van crowd. Overnight parking at Shute Harbour is very expensive.

Denis Crampton – England

Tasmania

It seems that it should be easy to get a lift on a sailing boat at the start of January because the yacht's are in Hobart after the races from Melbourne and Sydney. Many of the crew members fly home and the skippers have to find a new crew.

Susan Hâster – Switzerland

Victoria
Ballarat

Montrose Cottage, Eureka Museum and *Priscilla's Cottage Tea Rooms*, 109-111 Eureka St, Ballarat, are open from 9.30 am daily. Admission charges are A$3 for adults and A$1.50 for children. A family ticket costs A$8.50.

Montrose Cottage is a National Trust property with authentic furnishings which belonged to the original owners. It is the only miner's bluestone cottage remaining in Ballarat.

The Eureka Museum of Social History shows Ballarat's development from the Eureka period through to the 1900's. A friendly, informative guide helps bring all this to life.

L Johnson – Australia

We stayed at the *Sovereign Hill Youth Hostel* – what an incredible place! It's all brass and wood. We also spent a day at the government camp which surprised us. The bakery is terrific.

Sara Minkoff – USA

Echuca

Jack and Elaine O'Mullane run 'campanoeing' trips on the Murray River in northern Victoria. They will deliver you and the canoes to Picnic Point, Barmah and you can canoe slowly downstream to Echuca, exploring the waterways as you go.

The canoes are 4.8 metres long. Buoyancy jackets are provided with canoes and must be worn at all times. Cars can be left securely parked at Jack and Elaine's place in Echuca.

Two people plus camping gear and supplies can fit in each canoe. You pay A$30 for the first day and A$10 for each extra day you want the canoe. The address is PO Box 62, Echuca, Vic 3564.

Halls Gap

We stayed at the *Youth Hostel* and really enjoyed exploring the Grampians. The kangaroos at Zumstein's were really friendly. We also went on a hike from the hostel called the 'koala walk' and, sure enough, saw koalas lazing in the gum trees. The birds are fantastic.

Sara Minkoff – USA

Melbourne

We stayed at the *Youth Hostel* in Chapman St. Two days after our arrival, the hostel warden told us that a local warehouse manager had called looking for two people to work for two weeks.

We took the work – a great way of earning some travelling money and meeting the locals. We found short-term accommodation through postings at Readings, the bookstore on Lygon St in Carlton. We lived off Carlisle St in East St Kilda, a very Jewish neighbourhood. There are lots of terrific Jewish delicatessens, cake shops and small restaurants, not open Friday nights or Saturdays, but open on Sundays and the rest of the week. For fantastic cakes, we went to Acland St in St Kilda.

We found a great, inexpensive Lebanese place in Faraday St, Carlton and the *Shakahari*, 329 Lygon St, must be one of the best vegetarian restaurants on earth.

The old meat market has been converted into a craft market. Various artisans work on their crafts (basket-making, carving, painting, silk-screening, etc) and display finished work.

Sara Minkoff – USA

If you are staying in Melbourne for a while, there is *Ivy Grange* (tel 8619496), 3 Malmsbury St, Kew, which costs A$70 per week; the *Great Southern* (tel 623989) at 16 Spencer St in the city, which has rooms for the same price; the *Toorak Private Hotel* (tel 2418652), 189 Toorak Rd, South Yarra, which has rooms from A$70 per week; the *Regal Hotel* at 149 Fitzroy St, St Kilda, where rooms start at A$66 per week; and the *Hotel Victoria* (tel 6903666), 123 Beaconsfield Parade, Albert Park, which has nice single rooms for A$65.

Garry Blanchard

NEW ZEALAND

Air New Zealand gives 50% discount to those with student cards – you'll be on standby. Make sure you get your card stamped at a Student Travel office.

Michael Sorenson – Denmark

North Island
Auckland

I enjoyed the Hare Krishna restaurant, *Gopal's*, and found another gem called *Dominoes Natural Food Restaurant*, 2 Lorne St. It buzzes with a wide variety of music and students for the nearby university. They serve tasty vegetarian meals for about A$6.50, as well as pies, cakes, muffins, teas, cappucinos, and fruit drinks. Dominoes is very comfortable for a meal, snack, or just to sit for a while with a drink.

Megan O'Donnell – USA

Mt Eden

Mangawhau travellers' and backpackers' hostel, 10 Akiraho St, Mt Eden, has overnight accommodation from NZ$12.50 per person. The hostel has a friendly atmosphere and is close to a swimming pool and parks. Local calls can be made free of charge.

The house is a converted colonial home on a large section of land. There are four large rooms and a total of 20 beds. You can make use of the kitchen and laundry facilities. Guests are provided with a key to the front door and their rooms so that they can come and go as they like. We store luggage for free.

Simon Rea – New Zealand

Taupo

Rainbow Lodge must be the best place to stay in the country. Mark and Sue run the place and are the most helpful people you could meet. They'll give you information about the area and about trekking in Tongariro. They'll organise fishing trips and parties. Dormitory beds costs NZ$11, single beds cost A$22 and double rooms are A$27.

Michael Sorenson – Denmark

South Island
Christchurch

A new private hostel called *Backpacker's Hostel*, at 70 Bealy St, has opened. It is run by a few young Kiwi fellows with the intent, it seems, to attract those who feel YHA hostels are too strict with their rules and curfews. It's a nice old house with an outdoor gazebo.

Megan O'Donnell – USA

Picton

The Marlborough Sounds Adventure Company runs sea-kayaking trips with experienced guides. A standard touring kayak costs NZ$25 per day to hire and NZ$15 for each extra day; a sea kayak with rudder and storage hatches costs NZ$30 per day and NZ$20 for each extra day; a double kayak with storage hatches and rudders costs NZ$40 per day and NZ$30 for each extra day. Each group of people must pay NZ$150 per day for a guide.

Walking treks start at NZ$165 for two days.

Wellington

The famous *Beethoven House* is one of the worst places in New Zealand. Alan is constantly seeking war (thank God his domain is not too large) and he gives women a few hassles.

The place is dirty and always overcrowded. His information about the South Island is poor and not to be heavily relied upon. I learned the hard way. He does, however, cook good, cheap meals.

Michael Sorenson – Denmark

· · · · · · · · · ·NOTES· · · · · · · · · · ·

Australia

Adelaide The *Baukhaus Traveller's Hostel*, PO Box 241 Nuriootpa is recommended.

Airlie Beach There is a free campsite in Conway National Park, across the road from the national parks office.

BrisbaneThe *Yale Budget Inn* is now A$22 per night and is good value, despite the doors closing at 9 pm each night.

The Federal Hotel is now known as the *Spring Hotel*.

All buses now leave from the Roma St bus station.

Bicycle hire is A$35 per week plus A$50 deposit at Brisbane Bicycle Hire.

Mike's Kitchen on Brunswick St in the Valley makes great pizzas.

Great Keppel Island There is now a cover charge of A$5 at the *Wreck Bar*.

The *Youth Hostel* is A$6.50 per night and they're strict about chores.

Launceston The *Winnaleah Hostel*, Merlinkei Farm, is a fun place to stay where you can learn to milk cows.

Magnetic Island The ferry to Magnetic Island from Townsville is A$7.50 return.

Magnetic Camp in Nelly Bay costs A$5 per night or A$11 for three nights. Great value.

Melbourne The New Zealand Tourist Office (tel 6505133) is at 270 Flinders St.

Port Campbell The campsite costs A$6.80 per night in peak season and A$4.60 per night in the off-peak season.

Rockhampton The *Youth Hostel* does not allow people to sleep in their cars in the grounds.

Sydney *Sydney City Centre Backpackers' Accommodation* at 7 Elizabeth St (near Martin Place) has beds for A$8 per night.

Sydney Airport Backpackers' Accommodation, 46-48 Cameron St, Rockdale, has dorm beds for A$8 per night.

Kangaroo Backpackers, 635/665 South Dowling St in Surry Hills, is recommended

Geraldton The Swansea Guest House is now known as the *Sunshine Guest House* and costs A$15 for a single room.

Adelaide Newsboy

Noble Nelson at Trafalgar
pose on the streetcorner

Tacking down the tabloids
with one foot, tendering
the news with the left
pocketing and changing
with the right. The
lad giveth and the lad
taketh away.

A cheerful afternoon
entrepreneur, five
seconds in your day.

RUBBISH

All rubbish neatly ↑
secured

PACIFIC ISLANDS

COOK ISLANDS

Raratonga

I'm going to vent all my frustration and disgust of substandard 'budget accommodation' by criticising the *Dive Raratonga Hotel*, known locally as 'the Dive' because that's what it is.

It is unfortunate that a place like this manages to fill up every night. The people who run it will pick you up at the airport, but that's all you'll see of them.

They certainly don't come around to check whether there is enough toilet paper, dish soap, or other such commodities. The ancient washing machine was inoperable during my stay and seemed to have been that way for some time. There was only one hot shower and the water dribbled out.

'Budget accommodation', in this case, means paying NZ$12.50 per night to hostel owners who have more important uses for their customers' money than even the most basic property maintenance.

Megan O'Donnell – USA

TAHITI

Moorea

Guynette's Lodgement (tel 688375), Fare, Huahine has six double rooms with private bathrooms, a dormitory with a shared bathroom, and a kitchen available for all guests.

A double room costs 3000 cfp and dorm beds cost 800 cfp.

CENTRAL AMERICA

BELIZE

San José de Succotz

This village is one km before Benque on the way to Guatemala. The ferry across the river to the ruins at Xunantunich runs from there.

The ruins are worth seeing, but mainly for the marvellous view across the rolling, jungle-covered countryside. The entrance fee is US$1.50 and there's a tough one-hour walk from the far bank.

From the top of the main temple there is a great view.

I stayed with Ed Jenkins who has a place called *Ranchos Los Amigos*. It's one km further up the road from the ferry, past the village and the school.

Ed and his wife, Victoria, are the friendliest people imaginable. They are just setting up their business and currently have one cabin for three people and a dormitory for about 20. It costs from US$7.50 to US$12.50 per person and this includes breakfast and a huge dinner.

Victoria is a nutritionist so you'll eat well and Ed is an acupuncturist who will happily use his skills on you.

Richard Tucker – England

COSTA RICA

There is no need to show an onward ticket when entering the country anymore. A few hundred dollars and a credit card should do the trick. I came overland from Nicaragua, but did not need to show any malaria tablets and my luggage wasn't even opened.

In San José, the *Youth Hostel* is very friendly and hot water is available all day. They are a bit disorganised, so if they tell you there is no room, it is worth insisting that they recheck.

In Puerto Limón, I ended up staying at a place called *Pensión Caballo Blanco*, two blocks after the market coming from the railway, which is cheap at US$2.25 for a bed.

Buses from Puerto Limón to San José run hourly until 8 pm. The trip takes over two hours, but the schedule means that you can travel from Tortuguero to San José via Puerto Limón in the same day.

Paolo Lombardi – Italy

GUATEMALA

Tikal

The campsite now costs US$2 for hammocks and mosquito nets. For a small charge, you can also safely store luggage (as long as you've hired a hammock). The office is open daily from 7 am to 12 noon and from 2 to 5 pm.

Fresh fruit and vegetables can be bought at the Jaguar Inn.

Paolo Lombardi – Italy

The *Jungle Lodge* costs US$4 per person. The most popular and best place to eat is at the *Comedor Imperial Maya* where breakfast is US$1, dinner is US$1.60 and beer is US 50 cents.

Richard Tucker – England

HONDURAS

I did experience some very thorough border checks when arriving from El Salvador and when leaving for Nicaragua. Even if nothing suspicious was found, I was kept for an hour or more. Apparently, people from socialist countries are refused entry. Anyone arriving by air requires an onward ticket.

At the border with El Salvador, I was given a far better exchange rate for US$ cash than in Tegucigalpa.

Paolo Lombardi – Italy

We turned up at the Copan border crossing, ready to buy our visas – both the *South America on a shoestring* guide and the *South America Handbook* claimed this was OK.

Bribing and pleading made no difference. The officials insisted we return to Esquipulas and buy our visas at the consulate there.

As we were determined to see the ruins at Copan, we begged (again) for a 24-hour visa and, eventually, we got the 24-hour visa.

M Zantiotis

What I first took for men in absurdly large sombreros were actually bean and peanut vendors wearing the shop home after a successful day of sales...!

MEXICO

Telephone calls, international, are extortionate as you have to pay a 45% tax. Rates to the UK are US$7.50 per minute during the day and US$4.50 per minute at night.

Richard Tucker – England

San Cristobal

I took a day trip for US$7 to some Indian villages with an Indian woman from the tourist office. As well as visiting villages and churches, and explaining what you can and cannot photograph with your camera, she went into the history of the Indian people.

A group of us hired horses and guides from the Casa de Huespedes Margarita. Make sure you determine what you'll be doing before you leave. We took a trip to some nearby caves and were only 'allowed' to spend one hour there before heading back to town with half a day to go!

Richard Tucker – England

Nerida

The flag-lowering ceremony in the Zocalo at sunset is interesting if only to see the Mexicans attempt some pomp and ceremony. Make sure you stand up at the appropriate times or a guard will press a rifle against your cheek.

Richard Tucker – England

Palenque

The most unfriendly town in Mexico. I stayed at the *Hotel La Croix* for US$7. Electricity is extra but I was never charged for it. The *Casa Huespedeo Leon* is recommended for microbiologists and those interested in fungi. Richard Tucker – England

NICARAGUA

No one seems to care how many córdobas you import coming in from Costa Rica. Many men with gym bags of money will want you to change US dollars into córdobas at a good rate on the Costa Rica side of the border.

The problem is, you're going to be handed a bundle of at least 1,200,000 córdobas once you change your US$60 on the Nicaraguan side – do you want to be lugging around over one million córdobas, especially if you're just passing through?

Take lots of small US$1 bills. Cab drivers and hotel keepers are good candidates to change money with.

NicaTur, the tourist board, runs a nice shiny minibus between the border points at Peñas Blancas for US$1 for foreigners and 10,000 córdobas for Nicaraguans. When we were there, there was no traffic to hitch with.

Coming into Nicaragua, we had a minimal search. We left San José, Costa Rica, on a San José-Peñas Blancas bus at 7.45 am. The trip took five and a half hours and cost less than US$3.

You can buy tickets in advance, though the bus is not usually full. Leaving Costa Rica, we had to pay municipal tax which is about US$1.

The border formalities took about two hours, then we hitched to San José del Sur, a nice beach town and an intermediate stop.

Tom Harriman – USA

Buses are a total disaster and even Nicaraguans won't take them because they are so crowded, so slow, and such a hassle. The solution is 'el ride'. Yes, hitch-hiking is the way to travel. Taxis are cheap, so grab one and tell the driver to drop you off on the outskirts of town to get 'el ride' to your destination.

The taxi drivers will know good hitching spots. There will be a load of people hitching like mad and, sure enough, an army truck, a government vehicle, or even a private car, will stop and everyone will jump in.

We prefer the backs of trucks as you get good views and have other people to talk to.

If you're really stuck, a good way to travel is by taxi. When a totally full bus creeps by you and there is no other traffic, flag down a taxi and negotiate. You should be able to go about 10 km for every US$1. We also traded clothes with cabbies for rides.

Another form of paid transport is by truck – some huge old empty truck will pull up, announce its destination, and then you will be quoted some token price like (US)20 cents.

T Harriman & J King – USA

Bluefields and Corn Island

I wanted to fly from Managua to Corn Island via Bluefields and return to Managua by boat and bus. In Managua, I was only able to book the Managua to Bluefields sector and was told that there was a two-week waiting period to continue to Corn Island.

If travelling with a few people, hiring a light plane works out cheaper than scheduled flights as foreigners have to pay official prices for scheduled flights with US$.

The permit to travel to Bluefields and Corn Island is given by Tournica, the state tour operator. On arrival at Bluefields, I had to register at the local police station. This is normal policy if you leave the place written on your tourist card for more than 72 hours.

There is a boat to Corn Island on Friday mornings which returns on Saturdays. You have to book at the office by the harbour the day before you want to travel.

It's quite easy to get stuck on Corn Island as the waiting list for flights can be really long and the boat only operates once a week. There is also a food shortage and, unless it rains, no water, only beer (Budweiser!) and rum.

As many mainland residents visit Corn Island, the hotels seem to fill up a few minutes after the arrival of the boat. It's advisable, if you are travelling with others, for one person to leap off the boat and book a room. The *Captain Morgan Hotel*, which is nothing to do with Hotel Morgan, is good value at (US) 50 cents per person. It's clean and friendly, though the showers and toilets leave a lot to be desired.

It's no longer difficult to exchange money on the black market in Nicaragua, but it must be done discreetly. Unlike other Central American republics, it is not common to be approached by money changers in Nicaragua. It will only take a few minutes for you to find someone who will change your money. These US dollars are no longer destined for the contras. They are simply used by the locals to shop at the Tienda Diplomatica, where they can find a number of items missing from other shops. Only foreigners can shop at the Tienda Diplomatica and US dollars are accepted.

Paolo Lombardi – Italy

Granada

The *Hotel Alhambra* on the beautiful central park charges US$34 per night. The only viable alternatives are three blocks away towards the lake on Calle Calzada, and across the street from each other, namely, the *Pension Cabrera* and the *Pension Vargas*. Neither are very good but they are cheap, about US$1.50 for a double room.

There are ample restaurants in Granada. The *Restaurant Asia* doesn't serve Chinese food anymore, but it does have air-conditioning, great steaks, and cheap beer.

T Harriman & J King – USA

Matagalpa

Many travellers go to Matagalpa for some reason, probably because many volunteers work around here. Some beautiful hill country starts on the Matagalpa-to-Jinotega road. About eight km from Matagalpa, on the way to Jinotega, is the pseudo-German black forest, *Selva Negra Resort*. Unfortunately, chalets cost US$30. There are some nice walking tracks.

We stayed at the *Hotel Bermudez*, two blocks uphill from the eastern plaza, a little over US$1 for a double room with bath. The *Hospedje Plaza*, on the eastern plaza, looked a little better. The week after we were there, a Canadian woman and a Sandinista soldier managed to blow themselves up in a grenade accident at hotel. Don't take a room with loose grenades.

The *Restaurant Don Diego* has pizza and other good dishes on the upmarket end. Lots of cheap and good comedors all around the eastern plaza.

T Harriman & J King – USA

San Juan del Sur

Contra attacks seem to be ancient history here and there is plenty of transport. We visited this place twice. At 5 pm on Christmas eve, we took a taxi from Rivas to San Juan del Sur for US$3. Another time we hitched it and also took a reasonable bus from San Juan del Sur to Rivas. It is a real gringo hangout now, with plenty of beer, rum and good food.

The *Hotel Estrella* is great to look at, but it is slowly crumbling and there are no rooms with baths. Most of the rooms are set up for several people. Across the street with seaviews also, is the *Buon Gusto*, a popular place with travellers.

Two blocks east and one block north of the Estrella is the *Hospedaje Irazu*. Rooms with bath and fan cost US$1.

T Harriman & J King – USA

PUERTO RICO

I managed to rent a car on US$25 a day, which is quite cheap if you're sharing with other people. If you are not American, the people are friendly and the countryside is worth visiting.

In the mountains, near Jayuya, there is a very interesting big stone carved with inscriptions made by the Indians who inhabited the island before the arrival of Columbus.

Near Fajardo, there is a big camping place by the sea. It's uncrowded and you can camp or sleep on the beach.

Luis M Magalhães – Portugal

. . . . NOTES . . . .

Belize

Belize City Stay at the *Marin Travel Lodge* which has been recommended as being a clean, friendly place with hot communal showers.

Cay Caulker *Vegas Far Inn*, right on the sea front, has hot water and costs US$10.50 for a double room.

San Ignacio What used to be Jamal Cottages is now called *Maya Mountain Lodge*.

SOUTH AMERICA

BRAZIL

I found an excellent place to stay in Maceió, Brazil, called *Hotel Buon Giorno*. The rooms are simple but very clean, the owner speaks excellent English.

The price of the rooms is A$15 for a single or A$18 for a double. Considering the high rate of inflation in Brazil, the price is excellent for the type of accommodation.

John Rothschild – USA

Mark Balla, LP phrasebook editor, lived in Brazil for a year. He taught English in Recife, where he shared an apartment with another English teacher.

The life of a traveller in Brazil is a particularly pleasant one. Once outside the major cities of the south, prices are absurdly low. Dollars really do go a long way in this part of the world, and the existence of a healthy black market will ensure that this remains the case for some time to come.

What, on the other hand, of the foreign residents? Well, it is true that some of the more fortunate work for companies which are willing to pay in US dollars, but most of us 'temporary expatriates' see nothing but cruzados during our residency.

With the exception of the occasional social worker who manages to get work on a tourist visa, the only way to find paid work in Brazil is as an English teacher. Even then such work is generally restricted to private language schools. The major problem which arises here is that some of the schools are particularly bad. In general, the best place to get information on schools is through the British Council (not the consul), which has offices in Rio, São Paulo, Brasilia, Salvador and Recife. Otherwise it might be worth dropping in on any of the schools of the Associação de Cultura Inglesa (known as the Culturas), which are in almost all the major cities of Brazil. Both Rio and Recife have schools by the name of Britannia (not affiliated) which have good reputations.

There is no guarantee of work in Brazil. Trying to get a working visa before going is more or less a waste of time. Even those teachers I met who had work arranged with the British Council, had to wait six months before being told that the visa would not be issued. Needless to say they arrived from the UK without visas, and simply worked 'black'.

Finding self-contained accommodation in Brazil is no mean feat either. Some schools are able to arrange housing for their foreign teachers. The question which arises once a home has been found is how to live. A foreign English teacher in Brazil will have the means to carry on a 'middle class' existence. To understand what this entails, one must have a basic concept of the make-up of Brazilian society. What is it to be a 'middle class' Brazilian?

Brazilians (according to Brazilians) come in two kinds. The first kind – some 25 to 30% of the population – lives in a kind of mini western world, with a stratified class system which can be neatly broken up into 'upper', 'middle', and 'working' classes.

The rest of the population does not fit into that system. They are the people who survive from day to day. Some of them make a living by removing the covers from manholes, and selling the metal to the manufacturers of manhole covers; others clean car windows at traffic lights; others beg. Somehow through their ingenuity and their will to survive, they manage to live a far more fulfilling life than do the wealthier Brazilians. The entire Brazilian culture as it is today has its roots where these people have theirs. The music, the dance, the poetry, the football – even the great Pelé himself – and above all Carnaval – the greatest party on the planet; all these things are in the blood of the street people and the inhabitants of the favelas (shanty towns).

As an English teacher life is easier. The opportunities to revel in the creativity of the 70% are almost unlimited. Brazilian spontaneity can be enjoyed by anyone almost anywhere. On the buses it is not uncommon to see a number of passengers beating a samba on the walls and the windows, or even hanging out the door beating on the roof. After dark a parked car may become a communal percussion set, and someone is bound to be passing by with a trumpet or an empty can of Coke just waiting to be filled with pebbles and used as a maraca.

Most Brazilian families inside the class system have empregadas (maids). They are paid anywhere from US$40 to US$80 per month if they work full time (seven days a week, 5 am to 10 pm). The minimum wage is around the US$60 mark. It is true that Brazil is cheap, but not that cheap. Exploitation is the name of the game in the work force. No employer seems to mind that many of his employees can barely afford to feed their families, while he is gallivanting around Europe on his biannual holiday with the family.

A near total lack of social justice can be very difficult to reconcile. Many foreign residents find it to be the only thing which stops them remaining in the country. Many others have learned to live with it, and sadly others have chosen to become a part of it. Whatever you do, however, Brazil is sure to leave a lasting impression.

Mark Balla

Alan Samagalski has worked on several Lonely Planet guides: China – a travel survival kit, Indonesia – a travel survival kit, Chile – a travel survival kit, Bali & Lombok – a travel survival kit *and the latest edition of* Hong Kong, Macau & Canton – a travel survival kit. *Alan sent us this letter from Easter Island.*

Easter Island is a tiny speck of gaping volcanic craters, jagged larva plains and sheer cliffs that drop several hundred metres into the sea. Situated 3000 km from the South American coast it's difficult to comprehend how the world's most isolated island was even discovered by the early settlers let alone how a culture developed there capable of carving, transporting and erecting the giant stone statues for which it is famous.

Easter Island is one of Chile's biggest drawcards, coming under Chilean sovereignty in 1888 when a warship was sent to raise the flag and the few hundred Polynesian inhabitants became South America's first colonial subjects in the Pacific.

The tyranny of distance has been overcome by weekly flights to Tahiti and Santiago, and stumbling over the island's odd collection of tourists – groups of elderly Japanese, French and families on holiday from Tahiti, Chileans on horseback and the usual smattering of wayward Australians – is almost as interesting as stumbling over the statues.

Outside the island's museum a group of amateur archaeologists on a study tour from Sydney were measuring the eye sockets on the 'potato heads' – oblong-shaped stone heads thought to be the earliest carvings on the island. Others scrubbed the lichen off solitary statues in preparation for coating them with an experimental protective covering. Measuring tapes dangled from the islands only triangular-headed statue. Even Thor Heyerdahl (of Kon Tiki fame) was due back for another look around.

The South America Handbook said it was possible to walk around the island in two days, but said nothing about the chances of surviving such a trek. Unprepared for the formidable sun after a few days my face already looked like that of a shell-shocked soldier who'd just crawled out of a trench after surviving a minor napalm attack. The Easter Islanders are 'very nice' about getting you a horse – any horse – said the handbook. All those old cowboy movie cliches about nags and stubborn mules seemed spot on as I tried to drag the poor creature back to Hanga Roa, the islands only village, through a heavy South Pacific downpour.

The next day, the sun broke through and I traded my horse (it managed to get back alive) for a more trusty motorcycle and charged off to the south coast (a veritable graveyard of toppled statues) and to *the 'nursery' on the Rano Raraku volcanic crater, a quarry where several hundred statues in various stages of completion peer out over the island.*

Various theories have proposed that the statues were moved and erected using great wooden bipods, sledges, aerial ropeways, reed boats or with the help of extra-terrestrial construction workers.

Attempts have been made to prove that the original Easter Islanders were North African Berbers, Incas, Melanesians, Polynesians, Hindustanis, Greeks or Egyptians.

Up on the crater rim, surrounded by statues which bore an uncanny resemblance to Malcolm Fraser, I realised that Easter Island offers one of the last opportunities to concoct one's own wild theories about the origins of anything.

Isolation, mystery, the formidable climate – all those cliches about Easter Island are true. All you need is a trusty steed and some armour-plated sun block to deal with them.

Alan Samagalski

COLOMBIA

I attempted to tour the coastal area of Colombia by bicycle. On my first day, I was attacked by two young men, who, in the lull between passing vehicles, pulled me off my bike, beat me with a stick to the point where I was bleeding profusely, threatened me with a knife, and robbed me of my accessible cash.

This occurred on the main highway between Cartagena and Barranquilla in the early afternoon, near the village of Santa Catalina.

Apparently, this type of incident is common in the coastal areas these days.

G Bellach – Canada

It is delightfully easy to be vegetarian in South America. In Columbia, you can live mainly on fruit and eggs. We met several fruitarians who were in paradise eating whole fresh pineapples and papayas daily. Cheese and yoghurt are also expensive and good in nearly every country.

Mineral water, usually carbonated, and some bottled spring water, is available in every country. *Jugos naturales*, whole pieces of fruit blended into juice, often with water or milk added, are made everywhere and are nourishing, refreshing snacks or meals.

Since everything is sweetened, you must say you don't want sugar if you want the natural fruit.

Getting enough protein can be a problem since nuts and seeds are hard to get, except in sweets. Peanuts are sold in Columbia but are expensive.

There are walnuts for sale in Ecuador, and Bolivia has peanuts and brazil nuts. Eggs are prepared in different ways.

Cheese is abundant throughout South America, as is fish in the coastal areas. In the colder parts of South America, beans and soups are great but often have meat in them.

T Harriman & J King – USA

ECUADOR

I'm a woman travelling alone. I've had no hassles in Ecuador or Peru, the men are very gallant, but it's outrageous for a woman to be alone in Chile.

In Otavalo, *Hostal Los Angeles*, corner of Bolivar and Colon, is very basic and has no hot water. Single rooms with bath are available for only (US) 80 cents.

In Quito, the newer *Gran Casino* is much nicer than the old one. All rooms have private bath and hot water. It's a friendly place with rooms for US$2.80. Food is better at the old Gran Casino.

Keiko Ohnuma – USA

Galapagos Incorporated, also known as Economic Galapagos Tours and Galasam, is a company to avoid.

The former fishing boat, *Poderoso*, has been poorly converted to a passenger boat. We had no refrigeration for food, no shower (as promised), a drunken captain, and dirt and insects in the cabins. Also, the boat ran aground.

The tour company sent no information to us regarding flights out to the islands, not even the departure time or name of the airline. No one answered their telephone in Guayaquil.

When all the passengers walked off the leaking, listing boat, demanding a better boat or a refund, no one would accept responsibility or liability.

Bruce Silverman

We went to Spanish school in Quito. There are two schools and courses cost $90 per week, plus a $20 registration fee. School goes for seven hours per day. If you want to live with a local family, it will cost you $7 per day. The tuition is excellent and we were proficient in about four weeks.

E & C Washington – Ireland

Eight travellers have signed a recent letter regarding a tour guide named Pablo Proaño who operates from the *El Paisano Restaurant* in Baños.

Apparently, the guide took them on a new jungle route, but did not know the way and got lost a few times. He walked well ahead of the trekkers, leaving them alone in the jungle. A couple of people got lost because they couldn't keep up.

More than once, the travellers missed out on food. The guide threatened to abandon people in the jungle if they did not pay him more. Some of the people the guide had hired were not paid and so they left in the middle of the trek.

The travellers who wrote to us were not happy with the way this guide conducted the trek and felt he behaved in an irresponsible manner.
Apparently, the guide hardly explained anything about the jungle flora and fauna.

Quito

Wishing to make a call to England, I understood the clerk to say it was 2600 sucres for three minutes, so I deposited three 1000 sucre notes stapled to a form with the cashier.

After the call, I was pleased to learn that I had misunderstood the clerk and that the call was only 2060 sucres. However, the cashier only returned 40 sucres, instead of 940 sucres. One of the 1000 sucre notes had been unstapled and replaced by a 100 note.

Protesting in my poor Spanish was not very effective. The loss of course was only about US$7 but it was irritating.

Rowland Bowker – England

PARAGUAY

Asunción

You can change (US dollar) travellers' cheques to bills in a *casa de cambio* for 1% commission.

Cameras are cheap but the choice is poor. If you want to buy film, you're better off buying it before you go to Paraguay, in Buenos Aires, or a large Chilean town where it is also cheap.

Robert Shaw – England

PERU

Changing money in Peru is a real difficulty. Apparently the government is cracking down on black marketeers and when I was there the only place you could change money was at the border crossing point.

I didn't believe this when I was told, and wound up having to travel all the way from Tumbez to Lima without a penny in Peruvian currency. Even in Lima, I could find no place that would change US dollars. Eventually, I had to go to a gift shop and make a small purchase. The owner then changed a

Cuzco, Peru

few dollars for me, but only after checking me out thoroughly, to make sure I was not a policeman.

K F Schneider – USA

URUGUAY

Montevideo

The American Express office is open from 9.30 am to 6.30 pm, and the staff are very helpful.

The *Youth Hostel* in Canelones is the best place to stay, since it now costs A$1.30 per night, and non-YHA members may stay there for a few cents more. There are cooking facilities, a lounge, and information is provided. There is a curfew from 11 pm. During the day, the outside door is locked from 2 to 3 pm, but you are allowed to stay inside if you wish.

Robert Shaw – England

Tony Jenkins draws most of the cartoons that appear in our books. He is also the author/illustrator of Traveller's Tales.

It's early morning in Ecuador. Roosters are crowing, the sun is rising and 'Immigration' is just waking up – unmade bed and upturned liquor bottles in the corner of his concrete chamber.

'Buenos dias.' 'Immigration' smiles, scratches, screws sleep from his eyes, and examines your passport while his coffee brews. His eyes are as red as the wattles of the roosters he would throttle into silence if it didn't hurt to chase them. He is a man of few words, just groans, and he presses an exit stamp, salida, gingerly into your passport, then sits down on the bed holding his head.

A nude calendar hangs on the murky turquoise wall of the customs bunker, and 'Customs', a leering beer-bellied man in an unbuttoned uniform, leans out of the window. 'Buenos dias.' 'Customs' is interested in mapas (maps). Are you in possession of any? 'Goodness, no.' You are, of course, and forewarned. The maps are tucked down the front of your trousers.

'Customs' smiles and lethargically ransacks your bags in search of contraband cartography. The reason? Ecuador, it seems, claims as its own a large wedge of Amazon generally regarded by international mapmakers as being Peruvian.

All Ecuadorian-produced maps, however, show the tiny country bloated to more than twice its size with this territorial wishfulfillment. Only these myth-perpetuating maps are acceptable. Anything produced elsewhere, delineating a teensy Ecuador, are taboo, and likely to be confiscated.

'Customs' is satisfied, your bags are savaged, and Ecuador is now a memory. You are free to move across the International Bridge in Peru, stopping on the way to become a millionaire.

Money does not clink in South America. It is all bills, tattered notes usually of huge denominations worth pennies in our currency. A flurry of Ecuadorian sucres becomes a blizzard of Peruvian intis. You hit the Peruvian border beaming, armed with a bankroll that could choke a horse.

Peruvian immigration keeps a chicken. It roosts on the lone filing cabinet and parades around the periphery of the office pecking at cockroaches and beetles.

'Immigration' wears a gaudy sports shirt, track pants and sneakers. You respectfully request 90 days; he suggests 30. 'Is it impossible?' you ask. 'Nothing is impossible...' he says with a smile. It seems that 'Immigration' has raffle tickets for sale. A worthy cause is in need of support: The Los Lomos Sporting and Cultural Club – Youth Section is having its annual fund-raising soirée in a couple of weeks time.

A ticket will gain you admission. There will be music and dancing. Prizes are to be won! You are pleased to purchase a ticket. 'Immigration' grants you a 90-day stay, stamping your passport with a thud that startles the chicken. He returns the stamp and a thick book of tickets to a top desk drawer with a smile.

Peruvian customs is just across the road and is represented by a fairly neat old soldier whose very scruffy dog is sprawled across the doorstep like a mangy welcome mat. 'Customs' motions for silence and waves you through unexamined from behind his desk. It's his only piece of furniture and he has no chicken. You have officially entered Peru.

Tony Jenkins

. . . . NOTES . . . .

Brazil

Rio The best tourist information is available from Rua da Assembléia 10, 8th floor, tel 2977117.

Paraguay

A visa to enter at P J Caballero costs US$1.10. Apparently, it's cheaper still if you enter near Asunción.

AFRICA

BOTSWANA

Maun

Kubu Camp (address PO Box 487, Maun) is 11 km from the town of Maun, on the banks of the Thamalakane River. There are camping facilities with hot and cold water. There is a laundry service, storage facilities and a swimming pool. You can hire cars, boats and camping equipment, and there is a full-time bush mechanic working at the camp.

BURUNDI

In Tanzania, take a local boat from Kigoma to the village of Kigonga just south of the border. This takes about six hours and costs under US$1.

If you get there in the evening, you are supposed to report to the police station and sleep there. We stayed with some friendly villagers and this seemed to bother the Tanzanian customs officers.

Customs is in a small straw hut as you walk north into Burundi. Just before you get to Burundi (after customs), you pass through a village destroyed by Tanzanian customs for non-payment of bribes.

From the other side of the border, you can get a minibus all the way to Bujumbura. They will stop at Nyanza Lac for you to get your passport stamped by Burundi immigration.

Mike Lees – England

Lac aux Oiseaux

This is located in the north-eastern corner of Burundi and consists of three lakes renowned for their bird life; Lac Cohoha, Lac Riveru and Lac Rwihinda. You can get there by minibus.

At Kirundu, near Lac Rwihinda, there's *L'Auberge du Nord*, an excellent hotel which costs BFr 800 for a double room with toilet. For another BFr 1000, you can buy a massive meal for two, served at a table in the courtyard outside your room.

Further on from Kirundu, there is a Swedish mission where you can stay. You can walk to Lac Rwihinda from Kirundu and it takes about one hour.

Mike Lees – England

Muishanga

From Muishanga, you can continue on the road to a waterfall and hike to a gorge. You follow the waterfall upstream for about two and a half hours, taking the right-hand path. You meet the dirt track which has gone the long way round and continue to the gorge. You can walk down to Gihofi from the gorge in about four hours.

J Noakes & C Combrie – England

Muhweza

You can walk directly to the Source du Nil from Rutovu (unspectacular but nice scenery) or go back to the main road and drive or hitch.

Heading south, beyond the Source du Nil, is Muhweza and nearby are the hot springs. At the hot springs, there is a grass hut and a pool big enough to bathe in.

J Noakes & C Combrie – England

CAMEROUN

The people at the police checkpoint near Chad advised us to go back to a town to camp. Apparently, north of Waza there are bandits who will rob campers. We camped beside the checkpoint near Chad and had no problems.

There are many police checkpoints in the north and, apart from a short delay while they inspected our documents, the police were friendly.

CENTRAL AFRICAN REP

At Mobaye, there is an alternative ferry across the Ubangui River to Zaire. It costs CFA 4000 for a one tonne vehicle and CFA 8000 for a two tonne vehicle. Zaire customs are open on Saturday morning. When entering Zaire, a yellow fever certificate is required.

In Mobaye, you can camp in the grounds of the youth hostel, just below the Catholic mission.

Bruce Dougall – Scotland

EGYPT

There is a ferry from Nuweiba to Aqaba (Jordan) which costs E£33 one way. Visas can be obtained on the boat. There are two ferry sailings each day in each direction at about 12 noon and 5 pm.

Rosemary Moon – England

Upon landing at Cairo airport, the biggest surprise was that it is no longer necessary to change $180, or to fill out currency forms. The black market is dead. Since the spring of 1987, there have been two bank rates – the official rate of about E£1.75 to US$1 and the tourist rate of about E£2.20 to US$1.

This is an excellent rate for the dollar but, out of curiosity rather than greed (I tell myself), I ventured out in search of a better rate. On every occasion, when I quietly approached a store owner in private, I was met with terrified frozen stares, or suggestions to go to the bank or American Express.

Apparently, the secret police have arrested many store owners and now people are afraid to change money for foreigners.

Another big surprise was the relative ease with which Sudanese visas can be obtained in Cairo. Once you have a letter of recommendation from your own embassy (the Canadian embassy charges E£8) and present your passport and two photos, it should not take more than 48 hours before the visa is issued.

Tony Michel – Canada

Never underestimate the power of a student card. I made the mistake of not getting one before I left home, or before I left Cairo to travel south.

Perhaps the easiest place to obtain one is at the Cairo University. The student office is cunningly hidden, but any student will point you in the right direction. If you don't turn up with some sort of evidence proving you are a student, you will be refused at once.

The office expects a letter from your embassy, or some other proof. The infamous George can arrange student 'proof' as well as bank receipts. Somehow he has got hold of letterhead paper from British universities. For a fee, he will have an official looking letter typed up for you to present to the student office at Cairo university.

G Long – England

Alexandria

The *Youth Hostel* is a black pit of noise, filth and buggery. My travelling companion was nearly gang-raped when a frenzied party turned into an orgy. He only just escaped with his posterior virginity intact!

Mark Paules – USA

Cairo

I spent a night at the renovated youth hostel which is beautiful beyond all expectations – a Hilton among hostels. It costs E£2.50 per night in a room with six others. Breakfast is included in the price.

In each room, there are sturdy lockers into which you can force large backpacks. Lockers and keys are provided free of charge, but you must leave a E£2 deposit.

Tony Michel – Canada

The *Hotel Everest* has no hot water and the bathrooms are filthy. A single room with a basin costs E£5.35, including a somewhat dodgy, though filling, breakfast of bread, jam, butter, cheese, hard-boiled egg and tea. A pack left in the sitting room of the hotel lobby was safe for the day.

A limited but sufficient metro system has just been opened in Cairo. The fare is 25 pt regardless of the distance one is travelling.

Anne Boardman – USA

KENYA

In New York, visas for Kenya are issued within 48 hours. You require a valid passport, two photos, US$10, and an onward ticket (or letter from your travel agent stating that you have bought a return ticket). Other offices issuing visas for Kenya are the Kenya Embassy, 2249 'R' St NW, Washington, DC 20008, USA and the Kenya Consulate, 9100 Wilshire Boulevard, Doheny Plaza – Suite 111, Beverly Hills, CA 90212, USA.

Nairobi

We stayed at the *Iqbal Hotel*, Latema Rd. It's clean, cheap and always full of travellers. The people there are friendly, but don't fall into a false sense of security – my friend was assaulted near the Nairobi Cinema at dusk. No one came to help her when she screamed.

The best place to change money on the black market is at Zanzibar Curios, Tom Mboya St. Don't try to change money on the streets of Nairobi or Mombassa – you'll either be robbed or conned.

Simon Oulton – England

Eddie is no longer at El Kindly Travel, but his brother works there and refers to himself as Eddie. I booked a camping safari to the Masai area and was told I would be given a 20% discount. When I arrived to go on safari, I was told that the amount would have been refunded when he received his commission.

He used 'Travel Unlimited' to book two days over Christmas for me at the Nairobi Safari Club and charged me Sh 6000 for the two days. When I asked the receptionist about the daily rate, I was told it was Sh 2470 per day. Once again, I had a hassle getting a refund.

Next 'Eddie' booked me on a four-day safari, staying at the *Ark Mountain Lodge* and the *Abadare Country Club*. I was promised that the rates would be discounted 30% of the retail rate – more problems when the bill came.

Bill McDowell – USA

MALAWI

Blantyre

The *Rest House* is on Chikka Rd. The VIP room costs Kw 8, a double room costs Kw 6.75 and a single room costs Kw 4.50.

If you want to climb the Mulanje, ring 633157 and speak to Andy Crab or Mrs Killick.

Andy takes people up the Mulanje mountain occasionally, and he is a good guide.

Kim Kanger – Sweden

How to go on a safari for free. Bargain with the tour company. Hire a bus with a driver, but don't hire a cook or buy food. Arrange for a good reduction, then go to a hostel and gather 10 or so travellers. (Do not forget to mention to the company you bargain with that you will be finding another 10 people to travel with).

Offer the travellers a cheap safari and tell them they have to bring their own food. If 10 people pay Sh 200 each, you'll get a free trip.

Kim Kanger – Sweden

RWANDA

Kigali

The *Bienvenu Hotel* costs BFr 2000 for a double room and is a very nice place. The *Town Hotel* is nondescript and costs BFr 1000 for a double room.

Mike Lees – England

SOUTH AFRICA

Johannesburg

The people at the tourist office in the Carlton Centre are very helpful and have good maps. They seem to respect low budget travellers, and they think it's OK to travel on 'black' buses and 3rd class trains.

The people in the 'white' section of the railway station are very conservative and always recommend that you don't go 3rd class. 'You could get killed,' one lady told me. The people in the 'white' section of the railway station also apologise when they mention the Greyhound or Translux express buses because they are multi-racial.

The railway discount for tourists was scrapped last year, so now it's definitely better to travel by express bus. Travelling by bus is cheaper and much faster than travelling 2nd class in the train.

If you want to rent a car, try Rent-a-wreck (tel 402 7043). They have cars at various rates from Rs 15 per day and 15 cents for every km. There are lower rates for weekly or monthly rental.

The Soweto tours are supposedly very good. The new guide is a Sowetan and isn't afraid to tell the truth. The cost of a tour is R25 (R15 for students). You can book by ringing 932 0000, extension 2020.

Magnus Dahl – Sweden

TANZANIA

Ribondo Island

It would be great to visit this island in the southwest of Lake Victoria. It does not get any visitors for months at a time. Never made it, but apparently it takes two days to get there from Mwanza. A glance at the map makes you think it could be done in a day. Book at the State Travel Service in Mwanza, where they will radio the wardens to let them know you are coming.

Mike Lees – England

Tabora

The *Railway Hotel* is a good place for food and a shower when you're waiting for that train.

If you have a whole day to spare, hitch a ride and then take a four-km walk through the fields to the small village of Kwihara where there is a house once occupied by Livingstone.

Mike Lees – England

UGANDA

Kabale

The *Highland Hotel* will only take US dollars for rooms, but has good food. Next to the Park Hotel is a nice African-style hostel which costs the equivalent of US$2 for a double room.

Mike Lees – England

Kampala

You can camp for free in the car park of the swanky *Athena Club* where rooms cost US$70. An all-you-can-eat buffet-style meal at the club costs the equivalent of US$3.

The Shelly Apartments are now called *City Springs* and cost the equivalent of US$5 for a double room. Rooms are very nice and large but, unfortunately, you'll have to badger them for a while before they will admit to having a vacant room.

Mike Lees – England

ZAMBIA

The black market is thriving because the kwacha is worthless. At the Falls, just walk around looking like a traveller and you will be propositioned (if not, go to the craft stalls and ask). The official exchange rate is about 8 kwacha to US$1, while the black

market rate is around 20 kwacha to
US$1.

Tom Conklin – Canada

ZIMBABWE

Hitching between Victoria Falls and
Bulawayo is still not advisable. A few
months ago, a German couple were

shot by the side of the road and,
recently, a group of hospital workers
were killed.

A 2nd-class berth on the train from
Victoria Falls is Z$26.40. The
compartment is fine, but the journey is
long. There are six berths to a
compartment in 2nd class.

Anne Boardman – USA

. . . . NOTES . . . .

Algeria

Mali has an embassy next to Niger's embassy in Tamanrasset, and next to the
camping ground in In Salah.

Tanzania

Dar es Salaam The *Hajirah Restaurant*, near the old Telecom House, is good value.

The National Bank of Commerce charges Sh 26 for changing money – good value
compared to what other banks charge.

Uganda

Kabale There are several new guest houses to the west of the Capital Motel. The
average price is Sh 300 for a double room.

VISAS

In Kampala, Uganda, a one-week visa for Rwanda costs Sh 550 while a two-week visa costs Sh 1100. You require two photographs and the visa can be issued the same day.

The visa situation for Guatemala changes frequently but, at the moment, English people have no trouble obtaining one. It costs US$10 and takes about 10 minutes to process. I know a couple of British people who turned up at the border without a visa and managed to get one on the spot for a few dollars.

Some travellers obtaining Iranian visas in Pakistan have been given visas with a requirement that they change US$120 at the border.

The Mozambique embassy in Harare will issue visas to non-Zimbabweans.

When you enter Kenya, you must have an onward ticket or US$400.

To discourage the low-spending backpacker crowd, Burma has raised the price of a tourist visa from US$4 to US$32, and you must change US$100 at an official foreign exchange office.
  A seven-day Burmese visa, obtained in Kathmandu, cost Rs 85 in December 1987. The price of the visa has since jumped to Rs 695 – quite an increase which could stop some travellers from going to Burma.

In London, you can obtain visas for Madagascar (UK£20) while you wait.

British passport holders entering Jordan at Queen Alia airport in Amman, must pay JD10.75 for a tourist visa.

If you're flying from Darwin (Australia) to Indonesia, visas valid for one month can be obtained at the Indonesian consulate (tel (089) 819352) in Darwin. The address is 7 Bennet St. If you're flying straight to Kupang (Timor), you can obtain a visa on arrival at the airport.

Visas for Costa Rica are free for Americans, at least in San Francisco. Coming from Nicaragua, it takes only five minutes to get a tourist card at Peñas Blancas for US$2. There is a municipal entry and exit tax of 75 colones at Peñas Blancas.

Visas for China are easily obtained in Macau for M$90.

Apparently, authorities have been confiscating people's passports at the Central African Republic/Zaire border crossing, near Bangui. Travellers are told to collect their passports the next day at immigration in Bangui. Often the passports are not at immigration the next morning, so travellers have to stay another night or two until they arrive. Without your passport, you cannot change money at banks, or apply for visas at embassies.

In San Francisco, you can arrange a long-term stay in India without having to leave the country after 90 days by sending your passport, with two photographs and US$15, to the Indian consulate. Your passport and visa will be returned in a couple of weeks.

Australian citizens must have a visa before entering French Polynesia; a visa will not be issued on the spot if you turn up without one.

Sudanese visas now take 24 hours to process in Cairo, and cost US$10. You need two photographs and a letter of recommendation from your embassy.

HEALTH

There may be circumstances when water purification will be necessary, whether your source of water be from a country stream or a water tap in the city. The effectiveness of iodine in water purification is directly related to the temperature of the water. I have found the polar pure water disinfectant equipment to be a very superior method of water sterilization – Giardia cysts may be destroyed if the appropriate technique is used.

Acute mountain sickness affects different people at different altitudes. I have had friends become symptomatic at Cuzco, Peru as well as on the high altitude passes from Lhasa to Kathmandu (eg 5190 metres). Diamox (250 mg, three times per day) started the day before the high altitudes will be reached, and continuing the medication until the day you leave the high altitudes, may be very effective. In a group of 30 people travelling from Tibet to Nepal, with an age span from 25 to 82 years, none of those taking Diamox had symptoms of acute mountain sickness. There are minimal side effects – a mild metabolic acidosis,with some tingling in the fingers and the lips, possibly noted by some patients.

The recommended dosage of Lomotil for diarrhoea is two tablets with the first bout, and one tablet after each loose bowel movement (maximum of eight tablets to be taken within a 24-hour period). If the diarrhoea has not stopped after taking eight Lomotil tablets, the patient is in dire straits. Lomotil only offers symptomatic relief and should be used in conjunction with Septra DS. Take one tablet of Septra DS twice a day for five days, continuing even after the Lomotil has given symptomatic relief.

Many travellers will find that taking gamma globulin immediately prior to travelling will be helpful in preventing hepatitis. It is important to take the gamma globulin no more than a day or two prior to the onset of the trip rather than seven to 10 days before the trip as the effectiveness of gamma globulin is rather markedly decreased with time.

Dr H Parish – USA

I became sick with Scarlet Fever at the Evergreen Guest House in Jaipur. At the time, there was a doctor, a medical student and a nurse staying there.

I had a high fever and was sick for two days. Later, I went to Pushkar Fair with four Israeli acquaintances and got sick on the way. Seeing I was sick, the Israelis tried to dump me but I ended up in the same hotel.

They and some other travellers wouldn't get me a thermometer, asprin or any food. The Israelis left for Jaisalmer the next day and left me with a bunch of jerks (the hotel employees).

On the second or third night, the boy in the hotel brought me a thermometer and my temperature was nearly 40°C. Next day I was covered in spots and went to a doctor – the senior medical instructor at the Jodhpur Medical College. He said I had a viral fever and that I should have a blood test the next day (on an empty stomach) for malaria. He then gave me a prescription and the hotel owner drove me back to the hotel on his moped.

He sent the boy to get my medicine, but he took so long that the aspirin wore off and I started shaking. I took the medicine and my fever rose. I went to the hospital but the doctor didn't think I was that sick and he didn't have a thermometer to take my temperature with – luckily I'd brought my own.

The hotel made me pack all my things and threw me out when I got really sick. Nothing like packing your bags with a fever over 40°C.

The hospital wouldn't let me in. No beds. Finally, they doused me with iced water (using my own washcloth) and I slept the night in the casualty ward watching a guy vomit all night.

In the morning, the doors were opened and a pigeon flew in and threw nest-droppings on my head. A man was kicked out of one of the wards and I was given his filthy bed. Six doctors looked at me and gave me antimalarial drugs.

I developed blood-poisoning and was terribly sick for 12 hours on the day of discharge. They gave me more drugs and I gradually got better. I hardly had anything to eat during my two weeks in hospital. I paid one guy to do something for me and he ran off with the Rs 15.

The doctors eventually said I was fine and could finish my trip. I asked them if I could go hiking in the mountains and they said I could. I went to get my visa extended in Jodhpur. They sent me to Jaipur where the visa people were rude and wanted money. I went back to Pushkar, got a virus and was really sick again.

I got to Bangalore and the doctor said I had a cold. One month later, I got an infection in my saliva gland and poisoned one side of my face. As a result of being sick, I had kidney problems and some hearing loss in my right ear. Apparently, the infection in the gland was from eating coconuts and not brushing teeth regularly, as well as from being run-down. Everyone in Jaipur had sore throats and a horrible cough like me.

My parents panicked and had me return home. On the flight, the person next to me stole my onward ticket while I was sleeping. I had to pay US$200 to carry on to Minnesota.

Meanwhile, my mother is sure I'm harbouring some strange disease and threatens to have me sleep in the garage when I get home.

David Smith – USA

The following questions have been answered by the doctors at Traveller's Medical and Vaccination Centre, Suite 3, 2nd floor, Dymocks Building, 428 George St, Sydney.

What is Japanese B encephalitis and where would I be at risk of catching it? Also, many travellers I have met have received a vaccine against this disease – is it given routinely for any travellers from Australia?

Japanese B encephalitis is a disease caused by a virus which results in an inflammation of the brain. It is spread by certain mosquitoes and is prevalent in most parts of South-East Asia all year round. Symptoms include fever, headache, vomiting, joint aches and pains and sometimes coma, leading to death.

There is no specific treatment for this disease but there is a vaccine against it and it is available in Australia. However, the risk of acquiring Japanese B encephalitis, for most travellers to South-East Asia, is extremely small.

Only travellers who intend to spend more than six months in rural parts of epidemic areas, or those individuals planning to live or work in an endemic area for more than 12 months, should receive the vaccine. This can only be done through written requests to Canberra, via a local doctor.

At present, there are epidemics of Japanese B Encephalitis in Sri Lanka, Vietnam and Northern Thailand (Chiang Mai). We stress that for all other travellers, this vaccination is not generally recommended – personal protection such as protective clothing, insect repellents and avoiding being out doors in rural areas at dusk and dawn is still the best way to avoid being bitten by all insects – mosquitoes included.

Is it true that AIDS can be spread by mosquitoes, especially in countries like Africa where AIDS is so common?

There is no evidence of the AIDS virus being transmitted to humans by the bite of any insect. If this were to be the case, then one would have to conclude that only adults are bitten by mosquitoes.

AIDS is only spread through direct contact with blood and bodily secretions, hence it is spread via blood transfusions, contaminated needles or syringes, and through sexual intercourse.

Can you clarify conflicting rumours for the necessity of cholera vaccination for Thailand? I thought the vaccine was ineffective and rarely recommended.

The current cholera vaccine is relatively ineffective – it offers two to three months protection against the current strain of cholera.

However, not all health departments agree on whether or not this is an acceptable level, and hence cholera vaccinations are still occasionally recommended for some destinations, notably Pakistan and Central Africa, merely to satisfy regulations.

Thailand has not officially requested cholera vaccine for some years, and is not officially doing so now, however, there have been numerous reports from travellers who have visited Thailand after transiting through other Asian countries, that some travellers without proof of cholera vaccinations are being injected on arrival, possibly with dirty needles.

This is believed to have occurred due to the misreporting of an outbreak of infectious diarrhoea in Southern Thailand but, until the confusion settles, it is probably advisable to avoid delay and possible vaccination at the Thai airport.

I have been told that there is a major epidemic of hepatitis in China – is there any way of protecting myself against it? Do you advise postponing my holiday?

There is currently a major epidemic in China of hepatitis A – with thousands of local people having to be hospitalised. To be more accurate, the epidemic is occurring in and around Shanghai, and the source of this viral infection has been traced to a certain type of hairy clam.

Our advice is: it is unnecessary to postpone your trip since it is fairly simple to avoid infection. Simply refrain from eating clams and other shellfish; avoid water (unless it is boiled); ice cubes and fresh salads; and be scrupulous with personal hygiene.

The hepatitis A virus is only transmitted via faecally-contaminated food or drinks. Secondly, we advise all travellers to receive the gamma globulin immunisation just prior to travel as this will give good short term protection – even travellers who have recently been in Shanghai may benefit from a dose of the immune globulin on return.

There is also a high risk of contracting hepatitis A in Hong Kong and Macau and therefore gamma globulin is also advised for travellers to these destinations.

MISCELLANEOUS

In our last Update, we featured a few of the people who work behind the scenes at Lonely Planet. In this issue, we have Graham Imeson, Ann Jeffree, Todd Pierce and Richard Everist from our Melbourne office, and Elizabeth Kim from our US office.

Graham Imeson – Art Director

Graham Imeson came to LP by way of the UK where he was born. Between his birth place and his present place of employment he was waylaid in the US of A where he would have spent eight years in the shadow of Sears Tower, if it had been built at the time.

A brief sojourn at Caulfield Institute of Technology left Graham wondering what to do with a Bachelor of Arts degree in Graphic Communications. It was then that LP beckoned and in 1983 Graham woke up one morning and realised that he was head of the Lonely Planet art department.

In his old age Graham has become a model capitalist. He dreams of adding another VCR to his already impressive collection of three. His array of leather ties from all over the world is the envy of all leather tie freaks. He wears a Seiko digital watch and likes eating potatoes. Graham hates being picked on, which is probably why people do it all the time.

Ann Jeffree – Typesetter

With an interest in spending money as a lifetime hobby, Ann started with Lonely Planet in May 1987 after working in various sweatshops around Melbourne.

Ann is an inveterate traveller who, having explored the wilds of the eastern suburbs and ventured as far afield as Sydney, had never heard of Lonely Planet, and so was a little worried when offered a job at such a weird-sounding place. Since then, her worst fears have been confirmed – it really is a weird place to work. Besides all this (and more), Ann doesn't really want to be internationally famous through this Update, unless it brings a marriage proposal from a multi-millionaire. If you want to know more about Ann, write your questions on some good quality airmail paper, put it in a perfume-scented envelope, address it to Ann, C/O LP, and then burn it.

Favourite people: dogs and multi-millionaires

Favourite places: home (Melbourne and Sydney) and Candelo (look it up)

Todd Pierce – Graphic Designer

Todd Pierce started working at Lonely Planet in the winter of 1984 as a personal assistant to everyone (including all the existing personal assistants). He quickly moved up through the ranks to his current position of Graphic Designer. Todd has not travelled anywhere except eastern Australia. He has no hobbies, no desires and no dreams. He hates cooking, personal hygiene, country music, motor racing, football, and little puppy dogs.

Todd spends his nights alone in a pokey apartment in the sleazy Melbourne suburb of Richmond, watching old Star Trek videos. Todd is a very tedious person. If you ever meet him, tell him so.

Richard Everist – Editor/Promotions

Richard grew up in Geelong, Australia. His chequered career includes such highlights as painting ships (not an artistic endeavour) in Geelong, a brief run-in with the law (as a student of) in Melbourne, marble polishing (not the little round ones) in London, and working as a tripping counsellor (not that kind) in Connecticut. Somewhere along the way he grew out.

In between travelling and spending as much time as possible around the Otway Ranges he has been involved with the print media as a cleaner, freelance writer, copy-writer, sub-editor and editor.

He started work with Lonely Planet in late 1986 editing books, producing promotional material and working on the sale of foreign language rights. In 1987 he researched the fourth edition of Papua New Guinea – a travel survival kit.

Elizabeth Kim – Editor

Elizabeth joined the USA Lonely Planet office in July 1984 and became the first regular employee there.

Elizabeth worked half-time at LP and full-time at home on her own magazine of technology and human society. Her roommate was a phototypesetting machine named Sylvia. The finished magazine has since become an artefact and her hours at LP have increased.

Elizabeth grew up in the Hawaiian Islands, where she thrived on passion fruit juice, raw fish and mashed taro root, but she didn't go to the beach. She stayed in her room instead and read books about California. She stayed to earn her Berkeley residence: a Master of Arts degree in English Literature landed her a job selling costume jewellery.

If you like to cook your own food while travelling, here is an easy recipe for Palau.

long grain rice, preferably basmati
5 cloves
5 cardamoms
1 cinnamon stick
2 bay leaves
pinch of saffron
1 onion
ghee
sultanas
blanched almonds
half to one teaspoon of powdered nutmeg

Wash rice thoroughly, drain off water and dry the rice. In a large saucepan melt ghee and add cloves, cardamom, cinnamon stick (broken up) and bay leaves. Fry gently until aroma is released.

Put rice in saucepan and stir until the grains are covered in ghee (about two to five minutes). Add almonds and sultanas (you can also add peas).

Next, add water, salt to taste, nutmeg and saffron. Use the absorption method to cook the rice – use double the quantity of water to rice.

Cut onion into long, thin strips and fry in ghee in a separate saucepan until deep brown. Once the rice has cooked, place it on a serving dish and put the cooked onion on top. Garnish with green capsicum, tomato and cucumber. Serves four.

I seem to rack up a fair number of airline km every year and inevitably those flights provide some amusing experiences. Australia has some pretty strange aviation laws, and one of them is that Qantas (Australia's own airline) isn't allowed to carry passengers in Australia unless it's also carrying them to or from an overseas destination. Thus if you're flying Los Angeles-Sydney-Melbourne or Melbourne-Sydney-London, you are allowed to fly the Melbourne-Sydney sector with Qantas. If you just want to fly Melbourne-Sydney and nowhere else, you have to take a domestic carrier, Qantas can't carry you. Similar rules apply to other international airlines.

In December, I was flying Melbourne-Sydney-Manila with Qantas. Melbourne-Sydney would be a combined flight (a pseudo-flight I think they call it) for passengers bound for London and Manila. The London bound passengers would continue on the same aircraft, those of us for Manila would change. And the aircraft was going to be delayed several hours.

No problem for the London bound passengers, they would just have to wait, but those of us bound for Manila had an aircraft waiting in Sydney and couldn't hang around.

It was a Sunday and, by a fluke of the schedules, not only was there no other Qantas aircraft going, there were also no domestic carriers going either.

No problem, there was an MAS flight departing, we could go on that – if not for that rule about international airlines carrying domestic passengers. Before they can bend the rules in cases like this, Qantas has to apply for permission to the Department of Aviation in Canberra! So for an hour or so we stood in line while the department was phoned in Canberra, some civil servant was tipped out of bed we imagined, and after deliberating on the case decided ... no, we could not fly MAS!

The half dozen of us bound for Manila on that Sunday morning did make it in the end. We finally got on a domestic flight and arrived about 10 minutes before our scheduled departure. A Qantas bus whisked us from one terminal to the other and we rushed on board the aircraft, the last passengers aboard. Absurd? You're dead right.

These silly rules can also be manipulated the other way as Jim Hart, also from Lonely Planet, proved a few weeks later. Turning up at Melbourne airport for a flight to Sydney, Jim discovered that both the domestic airlines were out of operation due to some snap strike. Qantas, however, was still flying. But you can't fly Qantas on a purely domestic route, right? No problem. Jim bought a Qantas Melbourne-Sydney-Auckland (New Zealand) ticket. When he got to Sydney, he suddenly found (surprise, surprise) he couldn't continue to Auckland after all and refunded the unused Sydney-Auckland part of his ticket. Even silly rules can be bent.

In January and February, I was in Indonesia working on the new South-East Asia on a Shoestring and over that period made 10 flights with Garuda, two international and eight domestic. The whole time I was in Indonesia, the press was full of horror stories about Garuda's lousy service, incompetent staff, terrible delays, etc.

Well they made a pretty bad start. My first domestic flight was delayed five hours, well that's an untruth, it was delayed forever. They simply kept on delaying it half hour by half hour, until eventually we got around to the time the next flight was due to depart, and we went on that instead.

But after that inauspicious start they were always on time; in fact I flew out of Padang one morning half an hour before scheduled departure time!

But the most amazing thing about Garuda is their passenger loads. Apart from the first international flight Melbourne-Denpasar, virtually every flight was near empty. I counted 17 passengers on a 60-seat F28 and a mere 42 on a 220-odd seat airbus flying Medan-Singapore.

So Garuda flies on time but empty, and they also serve up (for their domestic passengers) what has to be some of the worst food ever carried aloft. And their booking system is definitely somewhat erratic. Garuda's Sanur Beach office, for example, did not even have a flight schedule so you are reduced to asking 'Do you fly from A to B?' They then call it up on their computer and say no! This method resulted in taking about one and a half hours to book three flights, all of which I later changed when I found an office which did have a flight schedule!

Later in February, I had the fun and games of trying to book flights during Chinese New Year. We warn people in our books not to try to travel in Chinese New Year since everything is heavily booked and prices skyrocket. Well I had to fly between Singapore, Penang and Bangkok during the week of Chinese New Year and Lonely Planet's advice was good. Everything was booked up.

After a great number of phone calls, Airmaster, my friendly Singapore bucket shop, got me to where I wanted to go but when I came to pay, the second piece of advice also proved to be true. Scandinavian Airlines (better known for flying Copenhagen-Stockholm than Bangkok-Singapore, but never mind) had bumped their bucket shop price up by S$20 (about US$10) in honour of Chinese New Year!

Tony Wheeler

We're still waiting to hear from John Stewart, our cycling correspondent, last heard of in Nepal, en route to the Middle East. Hopefully, we'll hear from John before the next *Update* comes out. Meanwhile, no news is good news....

Brian Jackson is looking for a travelling companion to travel through Africa with later this year. He is also interested in hearing from anyone who has already travelled there. You can write to Brian c/o PO Box 33-D, Fairfield, NSW 2165.

There's a company called Travel Secrets, PO Box 2325, New York, NY 10108, which will print out the latest information on courier companies in the US for US$30. They provide an audio cassette and fact sheets for US$16.

Some US-based courier companies are: Sky Systems International (tel (718) 6320566); Anspack (tel (213) 6493981); New Voyager (tel (212) 4311616); TNT Skypack (tel (516) 3384180).

Steve Lantos – USA

It's very expensive to travel in the Caribbean and many travellers can't afford to fly from island to island. A good way to get around is to get a temporary job with a cruise ship sailing out from Miami, or any other place on the Caribbean Sea. This is also a good way to get from North America to South America.

Luis Hagalhães – Portugal

The following information was supplied by the Commonwealth Bank of Australia and the rates were correct at the time of printing. These figures are not intended to be used as a basis for specific transactions.

US$1 buys:

Argentina	4.63 australs
Australia	1.34 dollars
Bangladesh	31.28 taka
Belize	2 dollars
Botswana	1.66 pula
Brazil	95.46 cruzados
Brunei	2.01 dollars
Burma	6.26 kyat
Burundi	115 BFr
Cameroun	266 CFA
CAR	266 CFA
Chile	244 pesos
China	3.72 yuan (RMB)
Colombia	272 pesos
Costa Rica	73.45 colónes
Ecuador	224.50 sucre
Egypt	2.23 pounds
French Pol	104.10 cpf
Guatemala	1 quetzal
Honduras	2 lempira
Hong Kong	7.79 dollars
India	13.02 rupees
Indonesia	16.65 rupiah
Iran	67.43 rials
Japan	128.80 yen
Jordan	0.34 dinar
Kenya	13.89 shillings
Macau	8.031 patacas
Malawi	2.54 kwacha
Malaysia	2.58 ringgit
Mexico	2245 pesos
Mozambique	454 metacal
Nepal	21 rupees
New Zealand	1.50 dollars
Nicaragua	70 cordoba
Pakistan	17.59 rupees
Paraguay	550 guarani
Peru	13 intis
Puerto Rica	1 dollar (US)
Rwanda	73.59 RFr
Singapore	2.01 dollars
South Africa	2.08 rand
Sri Lanka	30.84 rupees
Sudan	4 pounds
Taiwan	28.61 dollars
Tanzania	72.12 shillings
Thailand	25.22 baht
Turkey	1171 lira
Uganda	59.21 shillings
UK	0.54 pounds
Uruguay	300 pesos
Zambia	8.02 kwacha
Zimbabwe	1.74 dollars

Temperature

To convert °C to °F multipy by 1.8 and add 32

To convert °F to °C subtract 32 and multipy by ·55

Length, Distance & Area

	multipy by
inches to centimetres	2.54
centimetres to inches	0.39
feet to metres	0.30
metres to feet	3.28
yards to metres	0.91
metres to yards	1.09
miles to kilometres	1.61
kilometres to miles	0.62
acres to hectares	0.40
hectares to acres	2.47

Weight

	multipy by
ounces to grams	28.35
grams to ounces	0.035
pounds to kilograms	0.45
kilograms to pounds	2.21
British tons to kilograms	1016
US tons to kilograms	907

A British ton is 2240 lbs, a US ton is 2000 lbs

Volume

	multipy by
Imperial gallons to litres	4.55
litres to imperial gallons	0.22
US gallons to litres	3.79
litres to US gallons	0.26

5 imperial gallons equals 6 US gallons
a litre is slightly more than a US quart, slightly less
than a British one

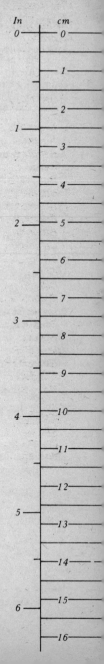

°C		°F
50		122
45		113
40		104
35		95
30		86
25		75
20		68
15		59
10		50
5		41
0		32

In	cm
0	0
	1
	2
1	3
	4
2	5
	6
	7
3	8
	9
4	10
	11
	12
5	13
	14
6	15
	16

Lonely Planet Guidebooks

Lonely Planet guidebooks cover virtually every accessible part of Asia as well as Australia, the Pacific, Central and South America, Africa, the Middle East and parts of North America. There are four main series: 'travel survival kits', covering a single country for a range of budgets; 'shoestring' guides with compact information for low-budget travel in a major region; trekking guides; and 'phrasebooks'.

Mail Order

Lonely Planet guidebooks are distributed worldwide and are sold by good bookshops everywhere. They are also available by mail order from Lonely Planet, so if you have difficulty finding a title please write to us. US and Canadian residents should write to Embarcadero West, 112 Linden St, Oakland CA 94607, USA and residents of other countries to PO Box 88, South Yarra, Victoria 3141, Australia.

Indian Subcontinent
India
Kashmir, Ladakh & Zanskar
Trekking in the Indian Himalaya
Pakistan
Kathmandu & the Kingdom of Nepal
Trekking in the Nepal Himalaya
Nepal phrasebook
Sri Lanka
Sri Lanka phrasebook
Bangladesh

Africa
Africa on a shoestring
East Africa

Middle East
Egypt & the Sudan
Jordan & Syria
Yemen

North America
Canada
Alaska

Mexico
Mexico
Baja California

South America
South America on a shoestring
Ecuador & the Galapagos Islands
Chile & Easter Island
Peru

Subscribe Now!

A subscription to the *Lonely Planet Update* will save you nearly 25% off the retail price. *Update* will be published in February, May, August and November. All subscriptions cover four editions and include postage (airmail where appropriate).

Subscribers to the *Newsletter* will receive the *Update* for the balance of their subscription. Check the address label for the edition number your subscription expires. Please keep us informed of address changes.

Subscription Details

All subscriptions cover four editions and include postage. Prices are valid until December 1988.
USA & Canada – One year's subscription is US$12; a single copy is US$3.95. Please send your order to Lonely Planet's California office.
Other Countries – One year's subscription is Australian $15; a single copy is A$4.95. Please pay in Australian $, or the US$ or £ Sterling equivalent. Please send your order form to Lonely Planet's Australian office.

Order Form

Please send me

☐ One year's subscription – 4 editions starting with the next edition. This is a

　　　　　　　　☐ new subscription

　　　　　　　　☐ subscription renewal for the Newsletter/Update

☐ One copy of edition number(s) ....

Name (please print) ....

Address (please print) ....

....

....

(Previous subscribers – please advise any change of address.)

Tick One

☐ Payment enclosed (payable to Lonely Planet Publications)

Charge my ☐ Visa, ☐ Bankcard, ☐ MasterCard for the amount of $ ....

Card No .... Expiry Date ....

Cardholder's Name (print) ....

Signature .... Date ....

US & Canadian residents
Lonely Planet Publications, Embarcadero West, 112 Linden St, Oakland CA 94607, USA
Other countries
Lonely Planet Publications, PO Box 88, South Yarra, Victoria 3141, Australia

C